Advance Praise

Prof. Achin Vanaik's new book while divided into chapters which at first glance appear to be disconnected in fact weaves a seamless web into topics which are of cricial importance to us in contemporary times. What was most satisfying was the Chapter which performs an audacious scrutiny of the Constitution of India. Our Constitution, even at the hands of liberals and radicals has been receiving uncritical widespread laudatory plaudits. It was necessary to perform an autopsy of this founding document to eke out its context and true implication which the book succeeds in doing.

—Mihir Desai

Senior Advocate and Vice-President
Peoples Union of Civil Liberties (PUCL)
India

Achin Vanaik has meticulously tracked the politics of the Hindu Right over two decades. He has done so with a rare and remarkable wealth of empirical material and a rich and wide-ranging theoretical apparatus. The present monograph is a collection of essays which reflect on Hindutva's typical characteristics, their manifestations in past and present times, as well as its projects for the future. The politics of Hindutva is then woven into a larger and interconnected understanding of several rather empty notions of secularity, of the possibilities and limits of nationalism and nations, of the contemporary phase of global capitalism which facilitates the present crisis. As counterpoints, Vanaik renews and enriches visions of internationalism and socialism in ways that are profoundly relevant for our present predicament. Meant as a warning and a message for the Left, this is a work that only he could have written.

—Tanika Sarkar

Former Professor, Centre for Historical Studies
Jawaharlal Nehru University

In this valuable collection of essays, Achin Vanaik brings his formidable analytical powers to bear on the challenges confronting India today. Narendra Modi's reactionary nationalist project, he warns, is well on its way to transforming India from a secular democracy proud of its diversity into a Hindu authoritarian state with democratic trappings, where Muslims and others considered religious and cultural aliens are relegated to second-class status. A key reason for the Hindu nationalist ascendancy, he argues convincingly, is the failure of India's liberal democracy to overcome the inequalities of class, caste, and gender that have been exacerbated under a regime of neoliberal capitalism. An alternative to Modi's exclusionary project is urgently needed, and the only viable counter-transformative enterprise, Vanaik says, is a socialist program that is truly democratic, egalitarian, and inclusive. Noting the current marginalization of the Indian left, he underlines the need for it to reinvent itself in order to be at the center of a revolutionary democratic resistance, and part of this process must be rescuing Lenin's revolutionary legacy from thinkers of both the right and the left who have conveyed the tragically mistaken view that it was the forerunner of Stalinism. While primarily addressed to the Indian situation, Vanaik's profound insights also speak to the challenges faced by progressives elsewhere at a time that the far right is on the rise globally.

—Walden Bello
Professor of Sociology and Public Administration
University of Philippines
Dilman

Nationalist Dangers, Secular Failings

A Compass for an Indian Left

Achin Vanaik

AAKAR

Nationalist Dangers, Secular Failings: A Compass for an Indian Left
Achin Vanaik

First Published 2020

ISBN 978-93-5002-655-7

Published by
AAKAR BOOKS
28 E Pocket IV, Mayur Vihar Phase I
Delhi 110 091 India
aakarbooks@gmail.com

Laser Typeset at
Sakshi Computers, Delhi

Printed at
Sapra Brothers, Noida

Contents

Acknowledgements

"Marxism and Nationalism" was a paper first presented when I was invited by Prof. K.R.R. Mohan Rao to deliver the Fourth Karl Marx Bi-Centenary Lecture in 2017 at the Centre for Scientific Socialism, Acharya Nagarjuna University, Andhra Pradesh. A duly revised text was subsequently published as a pamphlet by Critical Quest publishers. An earlier and much shorter version of the article on the Indian Constitution appeared as the cover story titled "Does the Constitution Deliver What It Promises?" in the May 2019 issue of *Caravan* magazine. "Two Hegemonies" is a revised, extended and updated version of a text of the same name published in the July-August 2018 issue of the *New Left Review*. Sections in the chapter on "Modi's Second Term" appeared in separate contributions to the *Jacobin* website whose founding editor and publisher is Bhaskar Sunkara. These have been revised and updated to become part of a larger and newer text. The final chapter on "The Question of Organisation" appeared in the July 13, 2019 issue of the *Economic and Political Weekly*. I wish to express my appreciation and gratitude to all those named above.

Introduction

All the essays in this collection have a common motivation—to better analyse and understand the reasons for the rise of the BJP and of the RSS and Sangh Parivar more generally in order to oppose them more effectively. How and why has this collective force reached the point where it now occupies a pre-eminent position in the body politic, i.e. it has secured a hegemony of sorts, itself expanding. The destruction of the Babri Masjid in December 1992 probably marked the key turning point in that it generated a much more serious and deeper concern about where the country was heading. This was certainly the case for all those who see themselves as belonging to the Indian left including not just the mainstream parliamentary left, but those outside it who have been sympathetic, hostile or merely critical towards that mainstream.

It was the growing strength of the Ram Janmabhoomi movement led by the forces of Hindutva that motivated me to prepare and complete my book in 1997. Abroad this was titled *The Furies of Indian Communalism: Religion, Modernity and Secularization* while the Indian edition was called *Communalism Contested: Religion, Modernity and Secularization*. Though the BJP entered the halls of state power in 1998 at the head of a coalition and remained there till its electoral defeat in 2004, the fact that what followed was a hiatus with Congress-led coalitions ruling for the next 10 years did lull some to believe that the worst might be over. This writer never shared that view and the return of the BJP with a single party majority in 2014 and then even more strongly in 2019 put paid to that particular delusion for many others. It also indicated that the process of constructing Hindutva hegemony has significantly expanded and accelerated.

My response to this more dramatic turn of events was to rework my 1997 text by substantially revising and updating it, exploring in some detail newer socio-political developments not accounted for earlier, and also taking up various theoretical debates that had emerged in the two decades since, particularly with respect to the discourses on the distinctive nature of Indian secularism and the dispute within the broad Indian left on whether the Sangh constituted a variant of fascism or not; even as it clearly had fascist characteristics of one kind or the other. The result was my 2017 book titled *The Rise of Hindu Authoritarianism: Secular Claims, Communal Realities* for audiences abroad while in India a slightly updated edition came out a few months later as *Hindutva Rising: Secular Claims, Communal Realities*.

Obviously this is far from enough and we need to continue tracking the course of the Hindutva project. Hence this collection of essays all dating from 2017 to as close as possible to the present. Moreover, the thrust and preoccupations of each of the essays here are quite different from those elaborated in the two 2017 books. The last decade has witnessed the rise of right wing or far-right authoritarian populisms of one kind or the other in different parts of the world including in North America and Europe. But the form taken by these populisms is everywhere an authoritarian *nationalism*. This is precisely why the first essay is on "Marxism and Nationalism". Marxists came late to the serious analytical study of the phenomenon of nationalism but since then have made notable contributions that need to be evaluated for many important reasons. First, to contrast and compare its merits to those of other, more Weberian influenced approaches. Secondly, this can help us to get a stronger grasp of the specific problem posed by the appeal of Hindu nationalism in India. Third, it is necessary for the purposes of understanding both the possibilities given by, and the limitations of, even the more progressive forms of nationalism and hence the enduring importance of pursuing a humane internationalism. This chapter is probably the most theoretical one in this book and is therefore of a more general interest to those outside India worried about their own versions of right wing or far-right authoritarian nationalisms.

The next three chapters more or less follow each other and deal specifically with the Indian context. The first of these takes up the nature of the Indian Constitution and, in contrast to the overwhelming thrust of all such studies by liberal or even left scholars, is much more critical of the Constitution's claims to having distinctive virtues particularly but not solely with regard to its secularity. "Two Hegemonies" is a comparative study of the early Congress political dominance and of today's Hindutva forces. It seeks to explain how the former paved the way for the latter and also what is distinctive in the way that the BJP/Sangh has forged ahead as well as in the nature of its ultimate goal. Whatever the compromises with Hindu nationalism by other political parties, the BJP/Sangh is the only force relentlessly pursuing the truly transformative project of establishing a permanent Hindu Rashtra! This chapter takes the reader roughly up to the end of Modi's first term as Prime Minister.

The next chapter brings matters more or less up to date. Shortly after coming to power in the May 2019 elections the BJP quite dramatically ended the autonomy of Jammu and Kashmir province. The grave implications of this act are duly registered. The Supreme Court as feared has sanctioned the destruction of the Babri Masjid allotting the 'disputed site' where the mosque stood to the Hindu claimants seeking to build a Ram Temple there. Since the late 1980s, if not earlier, the Sangh Parivar had highlighted three issues which it said must be resolved in its favour. Success in this respect would be a crucial marker of its political ascendancy and would constitute a huge and decisive step forward in its march towards a Hindu Rashtra. These were 1) a Uniform Civil Code (UCC). Now that it has succeeded in passing a bill criminalising Muslim men should they resort to instant divorce via triple talaq (which anyway had earlier been ruled illegal) it has basically got what it wanted. 2) Abrogation of Article 370 thereby ending Kashmir's autonomy; 3) Building a Ram Mandir on the plot where it had unconstitutionally destroyed the Babri Masjid. On the last two the Sangh has got what it wanted.

This book manuscript was finalised in January this year before the Delhi elections were held on February 8. The results there do not change the central thrust and arguments of this chapter on Modi's second term. But I take the opportunity in this Introduction to make a summary comment about its likely impact. AAP's victory in the Delhi Assembly elections in February confirms a trend displayed in previous state elections. Voters favouring Modi and the BJP nationally are more concerned about the development performance of incumbent parties at the provincial level. AAP's victory–exaggerated by the FPTP system–was because it was perceived to have delivered on this front. But here too, the BJP increased its vote share by 6 percent through a hate-filled, anti-Muslim campaign that denigrated anti-CAA protestors. AAP, which has shamefully supported the annulment of Art. 370 and the SC verdict on Ayodhya, deliberately stayed away from these Muslim and student protests. In brief, it will not seriously challenge the Hindutva agenda but try and skirt it by raising other issues. The short term and localised electoral setback to the Sangh is more than compensated for by the fact that AAP's unprincipled 'political pragmatism' indicates how the Sangh's more fundamental project of reshaping the very meaning of Indian secularism, democracy and nationalism has only gained further ground.

The last essay on organisation is, like the first essay in this collection, one of more general scope and interest. It seeks to explain why transcending capitalism is the necessary but not a sufficient condition for further following through along the project of securing greater and wider general emancipation from all oppressions. While there are a number of vectors of oppression, capitalism is a vector of exploitation and oppression that, relatively speaking, is more powerful and more flexible than other vectors in the face of progressive struggles from below. This essay seeks to trace a path to the goal of bringing about a socialist world order initially through struggles on the terrain of the nation-state but which must go beyond that nationalist framework since capitalism is global in nature causing huge problems that must be tackled at the global level itself. Today's capitalism constitutes a newer phase, namely that of a neoliberal form of globalisation. This constitutes a new 'system of accumulation' very different from the capitalism of the Keynesian and pre-Keynesian eras and is thus not reversible and not amenable to the practices of moderation or 'humanisation' that were applied then. Overcoming neoliberalism means overcoming capitalism itself. This would require such a great shift in the relationship of forces between capital and labour that the struggle to carry this out, if it progressively advances, would automatically put the question of socialism on the political agenda.

In other words, rightwing and far-right authoritarian populisms and nationalisms must try to present themselves as the crucial protectors and stabilisers of neoliberal capitalist ruling classes especially when they are being confronted seriously by forces from below. For us in India (and no doubt elsewhere) this means that the path to decisively and permanently defeating Hindutva with all its undeniable fascist characteristics cannot be separated from the struggle to bring about the transcendence of capitalism itself. The path to both ends is the same. This means the struggle will be a long and arduous one where success in achieving cumulative though partial reforms (despite ups and downs) will be the necessary, but again insufficient, condition for making the decisive structural breakthrough into a non-capitalist social order finally free also from any threat of Hindutva. The organisational question of how to go about doing this remains the key and is tied by an umbilical cord to a working class (in the broadest sense of the term) that increasingly recognises the need to overcome its internal differentiations, to develop its own revolutionary transformative vision that can then inspire it to collectively pursue the project of bringing about socialism.

February 15, 2020

1

Marxism and Nationalism

Nation and Nationalism

In the broad social sciences as well as in the discourse on politics, there is no consensus on how we should understand the nation—what its origins are, or on its meaning and value. By contrast there is widespread acceptance that nationalism—whether understood as doctrine, ideology, sentiment, identity or movement—is a modern phenomenon. But after this, agreement largely ends. Two central divides exist with respect to mapping the nation and hence its relationship to nationalism. Is the nation old or new? Is it predominantly cultural or political? That is to say, even as most would accept that the nation (and nationalism) is both cultural and political, which is the dimension that is more important for grasping its (their) nature? From these two basic divides in perspective stem a whole host of ambiguities of comprehension and assessment that has created a situation whereby all theories of the nation and nationalism are partial.

Moreover, given the multi-hued character of these two phenomena, there are overlaps among these different theorizations. So even as one must adjudicate as to the relative worth among these approaches and mark out and explain clearly one's preferential choices, it is also the case that among the otherwise dismissed approaches—dismissed because they are more limited or inadequate in their overall comprehension–some approaches nevertheless provide a deeper insight into this or that aspect of the nation and/or nationalism. To get a sense of just how complex these two phenomena are, and of the relationship between them, let us list some of the various questions that have been thrown up about the nation and nationalism.

Is the nation defined by objectively given characteristics of language, ethnicity, territory, history, etc., or by subjectivity alone? Does nationalism engender the nation or does the nation precede the emergence of nationalism? Is nationalism inclusive or exclusive? Is nationalism civic or ethnic? Is nationalism particular or universal? Is nationalism progressive or regressive? Or is nationalism all of the above in variable admixtures? Given these ambiguities it is hardly surprising that so many important modern thinkers from Marx to Freud to Weber to Durkheim to Keynes to Gramsci to Trotsky to Foucault have had so little to say about it.

So where do we start our exploration? The dominant current in the general discourse sees the nation as a modern phenomenon. But how modern is modern? Depending on how one perceives the background conditions and causal factors that have given rise to the nation, the dating of the origins of the first nations, ranges from the 16th century to the beginning of the era of industrialization. Of course, a whole host of nations and nationalisms only emerge in the 20th century with the rise of anti-colonial struggles. Insofar as the nation is both cultural and political, what distinguishes the modernists–namely those who believe the nation is a wholly modern construct–is that they give much more weight to the political dimension. That is to say, the emergence of the nation cannot be understood separate from its connection to the effort to establish some political control over a territorial space, i.e. autonomy within the modern form of the state–the nation-state or the multi-national state; alternatively, to merge with an existing nation-state or to establish a new nation-state.

Nevertheless, even among modernists, there is a small minority which while acknowledging the modernity of the nation, believe that the more important things that have to be said about the nation really come from addressing its cultural dimension whose roots belong much more to the past. In this respect they are aligned with those who because they emphasize the centrality of a cultural heritage of some sort to the notion of the nation, insist on tracing its foundations to a pre-modern, often ancient past. It is with this broad category of thought that we will start before coming to the modernist school.

Perennialism, Primordialism, Ethno-Symbolism

The views of some important representative thinkers are taken up here—notably Steven Grosby, Anthony D. Smith and Bernard Yack, each of whose views have powerful overlaps with each other and with various others subscribing in part or whole to this broad category of thinking. So much so that it is not necessary to pigeon-hole contributors as belonging to any single one of these three categories. This is why the subheading above refers to -isms and not to -ists. Nonetheless, for all that is shared across these three classifications some do describe themselves as being a perennialist, a primordialist and an ethno-symbolist.[1] Perennialism is a perspective that leaders of many contemporary nations have put forward, namely that their particular nation has in some essentialist sense been existing since time immemorial or at least beginning in some ancient past and surviving ever since through ups and downs that could include periods of submergence by 'outsiders' or by 'foreign rule', or once having a golden age but declining thereafter, but always capable in the appropriate circumstances, of resurgence, revival, re-birth! For perennialists the nation of today is a 'politicized ethnic-cultural community' of common ancestry and thereby having qualities distinguishing it from all other nations each with its own unique 'authenticity' and 'collective will'. In today's world most but not all of those holding such a perspective would be adherents to and promoters of an *organic* nationalism.[2] A few though might simply regard nations as perennial in the simple sense that they are persistent and recurring entities but not to be seen as 'natural' or organically distinct from each other. This minority might well accept that today's nations are best understood as the legatees of immemorial ethnic or cultural groupings which have always existed in recorded history and it is this legacy that makes today's nation immemorial. But all perennialists (and not just them) give much more importance to ethnic derivation than to modernist processes in explaining the emergence and character of the nation today.

For Grosby, the pull of the nation comes from its connection to the dilemmas of the human condition. There is a trans-historical need to locate oneself in time and space–the answer to the 'who am I' question. The need for a national identity is related to a human given–the concern for life protection, procreation and generational transmission. The nation then is like a kinship structure only wider, and created by 'cultural commonness' over a territorial space which in a sense is one's 'home' and 'parent', hence the terms 'motherland' and 'fatherland'. So 'the nation is a community of kinship' that is joined to what he terms as 'territorial descent'.[3] It is a 'social relation of collective self-consciousness' where that consciousness comes from *inherited* cultural traditions even if those traditions are *selected* and therefore vary as contexts change over time and space.[4] This shared consciousness is embodied in myths/ beliefs and symbols some of which will be rooted in material objects like flags or particular buildings of historical significance expressive of that community's unique history and culture. So the nation comes before nationalism which Grosby understands as above all a more recent ideology which reinforces a 'national identity' whose basic underpinnings are already there in that there is an existing 'structure of familiarity' that keeps away anxieties of behaviour through generationally transmitted customs, norms, values and beliefs–a habitus that routinizes behaviour and means one doesn't have to choose how best to cope at every point of time. This provides the necessary psychic health because it stabilizes one's sense of self which in turn is not separable from being identified with some others.

For Smith also, ethnic identity and community is the key point of reference. Yes, he says, there are both nations formed from above before the era of emergent nationalisms, as well as later nations emerging because of nationalism as ideology and movement e.g. so many of the Third World countries. But we must still recognize the 'cultural and ethno-symbolic nature of ethnicity and nationalism' and the 'recurring nature of ethno-symbolic ties'.[5] The older nations (most European states) have 'ethnic cores' residing in ancient or medieval times but this is also the case with nation-states like Israel, Egypt, Persia, Assyria and Greece with their respective senses of distinctiveness kept alive and sustained by ethno-symbols producing and maintaining an 'inner world' of national feeling.

Smith goes further. He argues that all nations today have four elements—community, territory, history and a sense of destiny, that is to say, a futurist possibility of greater fulfilment as a nation that therefore requires devotion from its members. But the individual strength of these ingredients varies. There is (a) 'ethnic selection'—the idea of being special; (b) a sacralised territory whose protection through the ages has meant that there is a pantheon of national heroes and saints to be remembered and honoured; (c) the nation had a 'golden age' of martyrs who sacrificed themselves for the nation and its future fulfilment/destiny.

Bernard Yack believes nationhood is old but adds his own twist to the reasoning behind this claim. All the above cited three (plus many more, including many modernists) want to understand why national affiliation arouses so much passion. Why does the nation as an imagined community cast such a powerful emotional spell that its members are willing to die for it? In this is it not like a family though writ wider? And insofar as kinship structures have long existed and are ubiquitous, surely the key to grasping its nature lies in its similarity to those cultural groupings of old? Unlike the modernists who insist that the nation is a modern social and political construct, perennialists, primordialists and ethno-symbolists insofar as they accept that modern processes have had some role in shaping contemporary nations, will nonetheless insist that there is the 'evolution' rather than the 'construction' of nations.

For understanding the nation, Yack replaces the idea of the community as a form of 'collective solidarity' or 'collective identity' with the view that it is based on a stronger bond of 'social friendship' i.e. it is a form of collective loyalty based on 'mutual concern'. Thus the nation is a moral community having a distinct moral psychology. It is an inter-generational community with inherited loyalties and because different communities have different things to share, they are different nations. Furthermore, modern moral concepts like popular sovereignty can arise with the advent of nationalism but they supervene on the essence of nationhood as an older form of community. For Yack it is the *fact* of being inherited, not agreement over cultural content, that is important. The nation is a 'cultural heritage community' and 'nations territorialize memory'.[6]

Strengths and Weaknesses

The arguments put forward by those who insist that the nation is a pre-modern entity has more weaknesses than strengths. But the emphasis on culture and on some kind of common cultural continuity from the past, i.e. an inter-generational transmission of 'feeling' has two main strengths. The fact of mortality is an important source of culture 'that huge and never stopping factory of permanence'.[7] For culture is the capacity for symbolic self-transcendence and can thus expand one's sense of being across space and time. So communities of belonging–and the nation is one form of this–can exercise an extremely powerful emotional pull. They help situate one's life, and more importantly, one's death as part of a wider flow of continuity and belonging–an uninterrupted chain of being! No wonder then that even those most modern of nations that cannot invent an ancient or medieval past (e.g. the US) will nonetheless seek in symbolic ways to 'immemorialize' their existence; to present themselves as communities of fate and destiny worth dying for. One cannot fully comprehend the 'passion' that lies within the national identity (and national identification) without understanding the importance of the 'cultural past' even when fictitiously constructed. This then is the first strength.

The second is that at least for some nations of today, an older history of cultural commonness, an earlier 'ethnic core' of some sort, has fed into the construction of the modern national identity.

Or, as many modernists would acknowledge at least for this small subset, that the past has been the necessary but not sufficient condition for their emergence as nations created 'from above' e.g. England. For such countries many threads in the nationalist discourse may be old but the overall fabric that is woven is new.

But now to the problems in claiming that the nation is pre-modern. The political dimension of the nation is, as it has to be, either ignored or greatly downgraded. It is only in modernity that a mass politics comes about as a matter of routine; and it is only in the modern era that there emerges a new principle central to all nations in their marriage with the state i.e. the nation-state—that of popular sovereignty. If once kings ruled, now nation-states govern. The 'people' (constituted as separate nations) are the legitimizers of public authority even if not the exercisers of state power.[8]

But even where the arguments for seeing the nation as pre-modern are supposedly the strongest—on the terrains of culture and identity—the problems are considerable. What distinguishes pre-modernity from the advent of modernity is that in the latter era, the rate, depth, scope, and continuity of change is so greatly different as to create another world altogether. The world has changed more in the last 250 years than in all the centuries before and changed more in the last fifty years than in the previous 200 years. By contrast, all pre-modern societies are more static and socially immobile. There is a basic separation between 'high' and 'low' culture and the latter itself is so localized that one has to talk of low cultures in the plural acknowledging its geographical dispersion and diversities of content. So how valid is the postulate of cultural unity in the past that is supposed to underlie the creation of the nation?

As for the claim that the nation is a wider community of 'kinship' can we ignore the fact that while the family and the clan are face-to-face groupings, the ethnie and the religious group are more imagined? According to one commentator, ethnicity has been defined in three ways: as (a) shared kinship and common ancestry; (b) shared occupation. These two are objectively precise definitions. The third is a looser definition open to subjective choice and means (c) any group having a shared identity because of one or more common cultural attributes.[9] The ethnie of the past, whether understood as small in numbers and highly localized or as much larger in size and spread more widely, either way the ethnie is definitionally *apolitical.*

National identity and loyalty applies to a population and space much greater and wider than the older cultural groups that are supposed to lie at the nation's heart. So how did the transmission of feeling from ethnie to nation take place? What particular traditions of and interpretations of the past get selected for generational transmissions? Who were the cultural guardians and interpreters among the elites? What were the institutions and mechanisms of transmission? There are two cultural attributes that have been more widely spread population-wise and spatially, namely religion and language. But here a 'reduction' of their influence is required if they are to be seen as key ingredients in the formation of the nation.

Is it not non-cultural factors like political continuity of state rule as in China or Persia that better explains a cultural or civilizational continuity? Yet despite a Han Chinese cultural continuity over the ages this alone did not create Chinese nationalism. Elite Chinese self-consciousness was not that China was one civilization among many and hence the progenitor of a distinct national identity but that it was civilization itself, the 'Middle Kingdom' between the Heavens and the Depths. It was the 19th century encounters with foreign powers that led to the emergence of a spreading sense of Chinese national distinctiveness to be directed against foreign impositions.

As for culture so for identity: modernity's impact on the structure of identities has been enormous and extremely disruptive. In modernity many more identities, not just face-to-face but also many more imagined ones, are created. Identities are sharpened and become more bounded. They are more fluid and dynamic. They can be intensely felt but are also more revisable. Identities combine and repel in new ways. There is identification with more impersonal entities–the nation, state, gender, race, humanity. This is the shift from closer relational identities to more abstract, imagined, categorical ones. Unlike the collective identities of the past which are mediated through particular groups and social stratums, the national identity is an unmediated, individualized, horizontal relationship. It is a new social imaginary. Just as the ethnie (here understood in the looser sense of a linguistic, religious, regional, etc., group) subsumes and abstracts from kinship, the nation—even when the ethnie is an ingredient in its formation—abstracts from the latter.[10] Isn't the modern personality a more self-reflexive one which more willingly *adopts* identities rather than having them handed down?

Insofar as modern processes create immense and unprecedented social upheaval, new social solidarities and new identifications emerge as psychic and social coping mechanisms. Yack's notion of the nation as a community characterized by 'social friendship' i.e. fellow-feeling is inadequate and far too sanguine. The content of nationalism is much more mixed and elastic. There is not just fellow feeling but because there are often competing nationalisms, there are strains of combativeness and even hostilities within particular nationalist discourses and sentiments. The reason why this is not perceived by those who see the nation as above all a cultural artefact is something they share with all those who give excessive and unbalanced weight to culture and see social order as decisively based on *cultural consensus* of some sort or the other.

A Modern Phenomenon

It is precisely because of its political dimension i.e. its relationship to the state that the nation (as well as nationalism) must be understood as a modern phenomenon. Theorizing must begin from this recognition. But depending on how one perceives the emergence of modernity—the weights to be assigned to the different causal factors—there will be correspondingly different approaches. Here the main divide would be between Marxists on the one hand, and on the other hand, Weberians/Neo-Weberians/Liberals some of whom may be unaware of their debt to the Weberian legacy. This broad group of thinkers is a much looser one having diverse views within. In explaining the emergence of dramatically new phenomena Weberians/Neo-Weberians do not primarily focus on production relations/surplus value/marketization. For them *changes in mentalities* is the pivotal mechanism. Since this arises from prior material changes and dislocations some would focus on this as a starting point for understanding nationalism; others would give greater explanatory autonomy to ideas or identity transformation for understanding nation or nationalism. Marxists can certainly appreciate the rise of the Enlightenment (of which Marxism and Liberalism are the principal legatees) and of the Protestant Reformation as contributory factors to the emergence of modernity, first in Europe then spreading elsewhere. But pride of place would nonetheless be given to the rise of capitalism and its operative laws of motion. Where Marxists would speak of a capitalist modernity where the adjective is of greater import than the noun, Weberians/Neo-Weberians and others would speak of a modernity that is *also* capitalist.

But there is no straight line from Marxism to the nation and nationalism; nor any specifically Marxist theory of the nation and nationalism as distinct from later Marxists providing valuable insights, theoretical and political, for grappling with these modern developments. What is germane is that given the diverse understandings of the emergence of modernity there are different starting points from which different attempts at theorizing have launched themselves–changes in social structure, changes in political structure, changes in political consciousness, changes in social consciousness.[11] Once again, partial insights are to be derived from the partial theories of the best thinkers no matter which have been their initial starting points of exploration.

For Ernest Gellner, the nation is a political entity that is functional for the rise of an industrial society where social mobility is much greater than in the past, where work is much more the organization of people and of messages (semantic work) than of things and therefore must rely on a context-free form of mass communication which in turn means a dominant standardized language of a created 'garden culture' (a 'national high culture') so a centralized bureaucracy can properly operate. Mass literacy and the development of an education system that makes this possible becomes a must. There is a great deal to commend in Gellner's materialist explanation. Eric Hobsbawm for example, accepts Gellner's definition of nationalism as meaning the process whereby the political and the national unit become congruent. So nationalism can take the pre-existing cultures and turn them into nations; it sometimes invents cultures and turns them into nations; or it can destroy pre-existing cultures and yet form nations. Language becomes standardized when there is printing, mass schooling-mass literacy. Nationalism and the nation are modern. Nationalism starts off being elitist but then develops a mass character to create political loyalties to an existing or aspiring state. It is nationalism that engenders the nation.[12]

But of course, in some cases like Serbia, Ireland, Japan, Finland and Mexico, nationalism pre-dates industrialization while in the era of anti-colonial struggles nationalism emerged in agrarian and even tribal societies. Given this diversity among nations and nationalisms, and given Tom Nairn's once Marxist orientation, he saw the *unevenness* of capitalist development and its industrializing processes as a major causal factor behind the rise of nationalisms. But the 'human material' of this diversity was an ethnicity preceding modernization and so different theories would provide differing emphases on the old and the new. That is to say, modernity and all that comes with it, is the necessary but not sufficient condition for developing a comprehensive theory of nationalism.[13]

In stressing the political nature of nationalism (and nation) one can go in any of three directions even as there will be overlapping concerns and some shared arguments. Nationalism can be seen (i) as mainly an ideology/doctrine, namely as a set of political principles; (ii) as an institutionally oriented movement where the key political structure or institution is the state; (iii) as a matter of sentiment/identity/consciousness when it becomes difficult not to give due weight to the role played by cultural processes.

If understood as doctrine, then tracing the origins of nationalism becomes an exercise in the history of ideas and their impact. The intelligentsia appears front stage and there will be an exploration into different types of nationalisms like liberal nationalism, integral nationalism, an organic nationalism, and so on. The contrast between ethnic and civic nationalisms comes in for scrutiny. Here nationalism is seen as a belief system of considerable shaping power over peoples' lives. It is something like a surrogate religion.[14] Elie Kedourie saw this doctrine as emerging from the philosophical tradition of the Enlightenment and invented in Europe in the early nineteenth century. Colonialism then dislocated the colonies in various ways creating among other things a clash of cultures wherein 'marginal men' became attracted to Western notions of independence and self-reliance thereby adopting and adapting the doctrine of nationalism to suit their purposes.[15] If Kedourie's approach ignored the earlier formation of nations as in England, France and the US, his generally more idealist approach to the fairly momentous historical changes that led to the rise of nationalism has made this starting point the least inviting of the four.

An exemplar of the second of the three approaches outlined above is John Breuilly. Like Kedourie, Breuilly emphasizes the importance of ideas not in themselves but in their connection to, and stimulation of, political action. That is to say, Breuilly highlights movements seeking state power which rationalize this search with claims of cultural distinctiveness that then require that an independent state be formed, or that the collective in question be united with some other state to which it should belong. Nationalist ideas and politics spread by *imitation* and are appealing because of the desire for self-rule and material progress by different 'peoples'. What is more, for Breuilly nationalism demands that the nation-state be the site of primary loyalty. The nation for many reasons must not be confused with an ethnie because beyond having cultural myths themselves transformed for contemporary purposes, it has a legal, political and economic character that is very much modern. That presumably most cultural of group attributes–language–is no longer just a repository of myths, memories, etc., but now serves the nation by becoming institutionally significant for law, polity and economy. In contrast, the 'Pre-modern ethnic identity has little in the way of institutional embodiment beyond the local level.'[16]

But though Breuilly does say that the appeal of nationalism comes from being a salve of sorts for the alienation that arises from the split between state and society itself coming from modern conditions of state sovereignty, bureaucratic centralization and capitalism, he does not source this appeal in nationalism's cultural dimension. Yes, nationalism must be seen as having a political thrust while an ethnic group unified by some cultural commonality does not *in itself* have this thrust. But that is no reason to ignore or even minimize the importance of that cultural dimension. Even a civic nationalism is not purely political for it does not require adherence to some specific set of political beliefs. So in countries like the US, France and Canada with a seemingly strongly civic-political form of nationalism, one can be a nationalist and a fascist or racist or a religious bigot. As one commentator has rightly said, 'All nationalisms are cultural nationalisms of one kind or another. There is no purely political conception of the nation, liberal or otherwise.'[17]

The reason why changes in social consciousness should constitute one's theoretical point of embarkation is simple enough. Given the diverse contents of nationalism, there is only one thing that is common to *all* nations/nationalisms. It is not religion, language or any other cultural ascription. Nor is every nationalism based on shared history or undivided common territory. New nationalisms or the desire to form new nation-states suddenly emerge, and if some were more predictable given longstanding tensions, there are others whose past realities of equable coexistence internally precluded such prediction. The fact that new nations then 'look to history' to present some characteristic as unique and therefore defining themselves as a distinct 'people', is itself reflective of a modernist outlook and sensibility. This postulating of a cultural unity all too often involves getting that history in some way wrong. The initial point of analytical departure then is national identity and consciousness.

Nationalism being a modern construct replaces the 'subject' by the 'citizen'. What constitutes the nation above all is that a 'people' come to believe that they are a distinct people and the factors giving rise to this collective self-belief are immensely varied. There is no common check-list of attributes or any irreplaceable or unshakeable ascription bar the belief itself. A nation emerges when a significant number of people see themselves as constituting one, and seeks political control over a territorial space. Since one is using the word 'significant' there is on occasions an inescapable vagueness in recognizing the emergence of a nation. This number may or may not be, quantitatively speaking, a majority. Its aspiration for nationhood may or may not politically succeed. A former nation-state may break up (Czechoslovakia) or merge itself in another (East Germany with West Germany to form the German Democratic Republic).

The nation is a state of mind but one with a political thrust. Since it is a state of mind, the nation can die out; it can be newly born; and is historically contingent. But how long it will endure one cannot say. The anti-modernist critique of the modernists is that the latter must assume that the nation would fade away quickly and since this has not happened, the modernist case for the nation is seriously flawed. But this is not so. To insist on the nation being modern and historically contingent does not necessarily mean that an early time-table must be put forward for its lifetime though it is true that many a Liberal thought nationalism would give way to universalism while early Marxists of the 19th and first half of the 20th century, being highly optimistic about the imminence of socialism worldwide, did think that nationalism would soon be succeeded by an ever expanding internationalism.

This recognition of the fundamentally subjective character of the nation and nationalism is why Benedict Anderson called the nation, not just one imagined community among many others, each distinguished by the particular 'style in which they are imagined'; but that the nation was an 'imagined political community'.[18] Quite the most accurate single line definition of the nation however, would be to see it as *a cultural entity lodged above all in consciousness striving to become a political fact*.[19] As mentioned earlier, this could be a striving for political autonomy or for separate nationhood, usually the latter.

Four Thinkers

Even among the modernists who have made identity and consciousness the starting point for their theories of the nation and nationalism, the divide between Weber and Marx remains. And it results in different understandings of how nationalist sentiment and feeling arose and spread; of its relationship to capitalism and modernity; in the identification and assessment of nationalism's virtues and vices. The two thinkers inspired more by Weber than Marx are Charles Taylor and Liah Greenfeld.[20] The two more inspired by Marx are Benedict Anderson and Neil Davidson.[21]

Of central importance to both Greenfeld and Taylor is the way changes that pave the way for the rise of modernity disrupt the human psyche and one's prior sense of identity. The national identity is a kind of salve that provides psychological well-being and a new sense of self-worth for the ordinary individual because there is greater public recognition of this identity that increasingly displaces the older stratified and fixed hierarchy of the complementary set of orders where the priests pray for the Lord God, the nobility fights for the Lord, and the peasantry works for the Lord. There is in place of the older notion of 'honour' and of 'behaving honourably' within your particular station in life, the growing acceptance of the principle of equal dignity of all. For as Greenfeld insists, central to the notion of nationalism is both the principle of fundamental equality of members and of popular sovereignty. The latter becomes the key legitimizing principle of the authority enjoyed by whoever now rules. The source of this new thinking must then be related to the rise of the Enlightenment and its expanding impact. How did this new sense of dignity arise?

For Taylor a stronger sense of religious individualism first emerged especially with the advent of the Protestant Reformation which had to, and did, affect Catholicism as well. This was later followed by a more secularized (de-sacralised) individualism which would give greater priority to the pursuit of human flourishing in this life. A new sense of time emerges. Time is linear because a new notion of progressive change emerges. It is secular because God's 'higher' time is no longer so prioritized. It is homogeneous because events now are seen to happen simultaneously across the now much wider imagined community of 'people like us'.[22] So Taylor sees the rise of cultural nationalism first among modernizing elites as a result of their desire for dignity in and through a broader identity because modernization disrupts the narrower social categories of lineage and clan that elites earlier connected to for their sense of self-worth. This generalization by elites of a new nationalist sentiment to create what (borrowing from Anderson) Taylor calls a 'social imaginary' comes about in different contexts. It can come about by (a) charismatic leadership (Taylor's example here is Gandhi in the Indian national movement); (b) modern processes of communication to generalize elite, concerns, hope, beliefs, etc.; (c) divisive action by minority groups motivated by physical fear against a hostile other.[23] The new social imaginary is no longer a hierarchical society where one's relationship to that social order was 'mediated' by some inter-personal web of relationships, i.e. the group or class to which one belonged. It has become a horizontal one with a direct relationship to the 'nation' as an *individual* and equal citizen alongside other individual members. This individual connection also means an investment of oneself in the national identity giving it a stronger hold in one's psyche. Taylor then, dates the emergence of the nation and nationalism somewhat later than Greenfeld for whom it is the emergence of the national identity that leads to modernity!

Like Taylor, Greenfeld says one must first historically reveal how the elite comes to have a sense of dignity and to see itself as a 'nation', and then how this sentiment gets extended to include a 'people. But she is distinctive among all modernists theorizing about nationalism in claiming that it is nationalism that is the real spirit of capitalism, the key factor in reorienting the economy towards the pursuit of growth. Nationalism 'provided a new set of ethical considerations and social concerns that invest economic growth with a positive value....'[24] Moreover, if for Gellner, the true subject matter of modern philosophy had to be the 'steam engine' (i.e., industrialization), for Greenfeld, the true subject matter of modernity should be nationalism. Identity provides a 'social map of reality'. It situates the bearer and gives direction for action. It shapes expectations for the individual and of others towards him or her and thus provides order in a chaotic human world. 'Both nationalism and religion are order-creating cultural systems.'[25] Among the multiple identities of the self, the one that is widest in scope can encompass the others and organize them within a more overarching and comprehensive framework. It is therefore the most *fundamental* and self-stabilizing of all the identities. This most important identity used to be religion but is now the national identity which bestows dignity to each member of the nation.

However, it is in her later 2006 study that she develops more fully her understanding of culture and identity and of the process by which nationalism surfaces. Here, she argues that what distinguishes humans from animals is culture which lies between the environment and neurophysiology. It is the process by which external stimuli are symbolized in the brain to create agency (will) and identity. What we can call the 'imaginative capacity of the brain' is really the cultural capacity to symbolize and it is this that creates the mind. 'Culture creates the mind'.[26] Unlike animals which are biologically programmed to behave in set ways in their species collectives, humans must search for cooperative models of group behaviour. Order and status, she says is basic to human nature, and culture-identity is the key stabilizer and ordering principle of a society whose primary role is to ward off anomie which comes from inconsistency in a human collective between different values, norms, perceptions of reality. An ordered society rests on cultural consensus and it is one's fundamental identity that provides that vital 'social map'.

Cultural change comes about when new sources of anomie emerge in different contexts and times. Anomie is caused by status disturbance among elites when social conventions that legitimize and prevent challenge to the existing order break down. The English and French Revolutions reflected this decisive breakdown leading to the emergence of nationalism which in due course as it unfolded worldwide took three forms. There is an individualistic nationalism–an association of free and equal members. There is a collective nationalism expressing a unitary will of some sort which can take either a civic or an ethnic form. What distinguishes each from the other are the different interpretations of the two core political principles, namely popular sovereignty and equality of membership. Authoritarian rule can claim to express the popular will, and equality of membership rights does not necessarily mean democratic rule.

But Greenfeld has also become more critical of, and disillusioned with, the supposedly healing qualities of the national identity. Her growing uneasiness with modernity now leads her to move away from seeing nationalism as the resolution of anomie to now seeing that 'nationalism inhibits the formation and normal functioning of the human mind.'[27] It can no longer provide a 'clear social map'. It is not a strong source of identity stability because it does not grow 'naturally' from one's environment such as those identities that would be connected to cultural 'givens' like one's birth, home, language, religion, and so on. 'There are far more people who are made deeply unhappy by the openness and pluralism of modernity than those who are made happy.'[28]

What are we to make of all this? Because Greenfeld reverses the proper relationship between modernity and nationalism (and national identity) she has to place principal responsibility for the former's failings at the door of the latter. But the disorientations caused by the enormous flux of modernity, as compared to the much more static character of society and therefore of self in pre-modernity, are due above all to its capitalist character; for it is capitalism that unleashes a dynamic of change that is permanent, rapid and exceptional in its power! What we find then is a new and deeper form of disorientation—a capitalist alienation. Given their frameworks of thinking, Greenfeld and Taylor respectively will place primary blame on nationalism in the first case, on modernity in the second. The result is a kind of shared nostalgia paradigm, a longing for the certainties of the past which presumably better secured the psychic and mental health of humans. For Taylor, religious belief is the necessary palliative today even as the multicultural nature of the world probably means that a system of nation-states will endure and the best we can perhaps hope for is a humanized and ecologically sensitive modernity. For Greenfeld the dilemma is deeper for it is unclear what other identity can replace the national as the stabilizing 'central mental process' or 'central "organ" of the mind'.[29] Neither sees transcending capitalism as the way forward.

Both these thinkers fuse culture with society and see the former as the more important term. Society is seen not so much as a nexus of economic, political and cultural-ideological relationships but as above all a 'meaning system' which can be best deciphered by grasping its principal cultural code. This kind of approach to understanding the sources of social order makes cultural consensus the key organizer and stabilizer. This is, in my view, an unbalanced culturalism. The search for the sources of order or stability in a society must be conducted at the level of the *social* itself, or in the socio-cultural system as a whole, and not purely or primarily at the level of the cultural system. Social order is not a simple or straightforward function of meaning. It has as much, if not more, to do with issues of power, and therefore with matters of social tension, dominance and conflict, as it has to do with issues of cultural and moral norms, values and beliefs.

There are four sources which combine in variant ways to maintain social order—culture/custom, exchange or rational choice, coercion, and finally, the *lack* of unified dissensus where the case for seeing widespread and pervasive dissensus is as strong as the claims made for perceiving a cultural consensus. It can be argued that in modern societies there are many more options of all kinds and that which keeps a society in some sense together, is not consensus but the lack of a unified dissensus, i.e. the absence of a counter-consensus challenging the social order. For normal functioning, active agreement is not necessary. Passive acceptance of the existing order of things is enough. The weakness of negative factors is more relevant to the explanation of social normality and order than the strength of positive ones.[30]

The original spur to Benedict Anderson's 1983 study, *Imagined Communities* (subsequently extended in a 1991 edition) was the outbreak of fratricidal wars between 'socialist countries', above all in Indochina. The practice by these states of 'socialism in one country' was bad enough and self-serving in the political-diplomatic arena of geo-politics but waging actual wars against each other was something else! This led Anderson to see nationalism as a sentiment and sense of loyalty somewhat akin to an extended kinship but more like a religion which is generally more inclusive than any extended kinship even. Marxists, he felt, had not grasped the importance of the 'sacred' and its connection to the problem of finitude and mortality. Nationalism had in some sense become a replacement for religious loyalties. There was a decline of the great unifying belief systems of Christendom and Islam while the elite self-absorption of the 'Middle Kingdom' was being shaken by the widened horizons resulting from the explorations of the non-European and Arab worlds. The 'sacred' languages of Latin and Quranic Arabic which were supposed to give access to 'religious truth' were being demoted in importance, while Chinese encounters with more powerful outsiders were eroding the self-confidence of the Chinese imperial bureaucracy whose internal coherence was based on the 'Mandarinate system'. In addition, other cultural de-stabilizers were the emergence of (a) new concepts of social equality and growing questioning of the view that social hierarchy and complementarity of functions was natural and God given; (b) a separation of cosmological and human historical time with concern over the latter becoming increasingly important since there was available a new awareness of possible cumulative progress in this life. That is to say, there were new ways in which fraternity, power and time could be linked. For Anderson then, the nation is the modern secular version of the 'sacred' community.

As a modernist and Marxist, Anderson sought to connect the rise of nationalism to capitalism. Here, he highlighted the importance of print-capitalism and standardized print-languages of the non-sacred vernaculars in explaining the spread of the idea of nationalism from elites to masses. The 'horizontal comradeship' of the nation is created by all kinds of artefacts in the form of symbols, poems, plays, stories, pictures, buildings of the new 'collective'. State activities also contributed the forging of this national consciousness through censuses, maps, museums and through its administrative routines.

Though Anderson is emphatic that the nation is very much a political community, his is primarily an exploration into the culturally imagined character of the nation. Valuable as this is, it leaves a great deal out. The 'emotional unification' of the imagined nation is not just a product of cultural activities but there also has to be a constructed separation from other nations where the political and the extra-national must come in. Cultural-emotional unity alone does not a nation make. That group has to be politicized; there has to be a striving for some specifically political end. It is a grouping operating in those 'political fields' concerned with the 'conditions and transformations that created modern nation-states'.[31] One such field is that of external conflict and war and therefore nationalism is connected to the study of the economic and social history of the nation-state in a wider context of transnational processes of *inter*-nationalism.[32]

Like Anderson, Neil Davidson also sees the nation as subjectively defined but nationalisms for him are differentiated more by their differing relationships to 'external social reality' than by different 'styles of imagining'. There is a difference of emphasis between these two Marxist thinkers. Davidson insists that sharing a cultural attribute of some sort does not alone make for a distinctive sense of the collective-self. For that there has to be a *contrast* with some other group, community or nation. This is a sensible enough caution but more debatable is his insistence that national consciousness must be separated from having a national identity. The former is an 'internal psychological state' while the latter is necessarily an external relation or contrastive state which has to have some signs or markers showing to one-self and others that one *holds* to a particular identity. This is unconvincing. One can with as much plausibility argue that a 'national' consciousness is also a contrastive state. But by making this separation Davidson wants to claim that while a national consciousness may have emerged earlier, it is capitalism that 'crystallizes' a national consciousness from prior disparate elements. This then allows him to argue that national identity and therefore nations and nationalism come about as the capitalist mode of production becomes stronger and then dominant. So a national consciousness emerges unevenly across Europe (1450-1688) among certain elite groups; it spreads to other parts of Europe and to North America (1688-1789); and then there is diffusion to the masses (1789-1848). On the one hand Davidson wants to tie the rise of the early nations in Europe (England and France) as strongly as he can to the rise of capitalism as the main mode of production. On the other hand, he insists that the emergence of capitalism must be tied to the bourgeois revolutions in England and France.

The dating of the origins of capitalism thus becomes important for Marxists because they seek to connect the first nationalism in England to this origin. Greenfeld though a modernist says national identity/nationalism first arises in the very period of the 15th and 16th century which for Davidson designates the time when national consciousness emerges. Robert Brenner and the school of 'Political Marxists' he inspired provides a way of reconciling the partial claims of both Davidson and Greenfeld. Political Marxists can agree with those who trace the rise of a sense of nationhood in England to the early 16th century and yet insist that this was tied to the rise of capitalism precisely because capitalist social relations first arose in the first half of the 16th century. Political Marxists reject the argument that the bourgeois revolution of the 17th century in England was the necessary pre-condition for the capitalist mode of production to make the crucial breakthrough to becoming the dominant mode.[33]

Where Davidson and other Marxists are on strong grounds is in arguing that the rise of capitalism created a much more complex society in which the rising class, the bourgeoisie needed a new social glue, namely nationalism, to sustain its rule over the lower orders. Industrialization and urbanization create new and highly disruptive life experiences resulting in new psychological needs where nationalism provides a form of psychic compensation in the face of growing uncertainties and newer and more generalized forms of alienation. The particular merit of Davidson's intervention into the debate is that he highlights the functional importance of nationalism for class domination! Nationalism provides psychic compensation for alienation not assuage-able by consumption. It mobilizes working classes for 'our' ruling classes against 'other' ruling classes. He does well to remind us that while there are limits to how radically progressive nationalism can be, there are no limits to how reactionary it can be.[34]

Marxist Legacies

It is only in the last quarter of the 20th century that Marxist intellectuals began to address the issue of nationalism with the seriousness it deserved. Before that, the Marxist legacy of thought on this issue dating from the work of Marx and Engels themselves was incomplete, contradictory and ambiguous. Common to all the different currents within this tradition–Marx and Engels, the Austro-Marxists like Otto Bauer and Karl Renner, then Luxemburg, Lenin and Stalin–was that the 'national question' (as it was called) properly belonged to the period of the transition to capitalism and of its further development till that stage was transcended with the coming of the socialist revolution and its subsequent spread internationally. On the one hand classical Marxism held that capitalism needed, and would in many cases get, the politically unified and solidified national territories it required for the free movement of goods, capital, labour for large-scale production and mass distribution of commodities. On the other hand, in capitalism 'all that is solid melts into the air' meaning that powerful processes would be unleashed which would erode national boundaries and cultures. The latter was more likely not only or merely because of capitalism's internal dynamic but because the rising power of the working class in bourgeois states meant the strong likelihood (though not certainty) of successful proletarian revolutions that would lead to territorial, cultural, political, economic cosmopolitanism.[35] This confidence about reaching the desired goal was widely shared even as different currents within classical Marxism did subscribe to different time-scales for eventually reaching this end; and even about how the national question might be resolved, whether under bourgeois or working class leadership.

Marx and Engels, the Austro-Marxists

Marx and Engels believed in sharp binaries. Nationalisms were good or bad; there were 'historic' and non-historic' peoples, 'developed' nations and 'undeveloped' nations, 'live' and 'dying' nationalities, 'revolutionary' and 'non-revolutionary' peoples, 'broken' and 'unbroken' nations.[36] Everything was to be judged according to the criteria of whether or not they constituted progressive peoples and struggles, where progressive struggles meant these had to be either against feudal absolutisms (accordingly M and E supported the Poles) or against capitalism where it had entrenched itself in Britain (here M and E supported the Irish).[37] That is to say, one needed to support the struggles of the progressive bourgeoisie to create the conditions for capitalist development where this was required; and for weakening capitalist dominance where this was possible. In the first case, which then were the terrains and peoples that had the capacity to so develop? Here Marx and Engels distinguished between large and small nations, between those peoples which had a larger or more recent or more continuous history of statehood and therefore higher potential to develop along properly capitalist lines than other 'backward' ones which would have to be absorbed by their more 'civilized' neighbours. Germany, Poland, Hungary, Italy had states—they were historic nations. Serbs, Croats, Basques, Czechs, Slovaks were non-historic peoples.

Given this one-sidedness in their understanding of nationalism it is hardly surprising that the Marx of *The Communist Manifesto* would declare that the advanced capitalist countries were showing the 'mirror of the future' to the colonized countries, or that Marx and Engels would welcome the French conquest of Algeria (1830-47) and the US invasion of Mexico (1845-7).[38] Yet in the *Manifesto* Marx also declared that 'working men have no country' but 'must constitute itself as the nation' to achieve 'political supremacy'. Subsequent writing made it clear that by this he meant that proletarians in France must be prepared to wage a war of national defence against the Holy Alliance (Prussia, the Austrian and Russian empires later joined by monarchical France) while revolutionary democrats in Germany should wage a similar defensive 'revolutionary nationalism' against foreign intervention. In both cases the pre-condition for success was an alliance with the peasantry and middle classes. In the justified criticisms of Marx and Engels on nationalism and their dismissal of the peasantry as something of a doomed class, this insight is often forgotten.[39]

Austro-Marxists like Otto Bauer and Karl Renner in their understanding of how nations and nationalities were formed gave more importance than other Marxists of their time (and Marx and Engels) to matters of culture and community going beyond the common recognition of the importance of language or of the level of economic development. Bauer, the most representative figure of the Austro-Marxists, took the view that corresponding to a given mode of production would be a specific mental culture which along with heredity created common traits passed on by law and custom. This tendency to tie nationalism to personality simply as a matter of culture is best resisted. But his emphasis on the cultural dimension had the real merit of recognizing, more than his contemporaries, the significant power of the nationalist appeal. Bauer believed capitalism produces a *nationally* conscious working class and not only a *class* conscious one. In fact the nation's shared history and culture could make that more powerful than class bonds. It followed that one would have to deal with the fact of there being a 'national character' and not just a class character to nationalism.[40] Nor did the Austro-Marxists think that the overthrow of capitalism would lead to an easy cosmopolitanism. Yes, capitalism restricted the cultural development and flourishing of the working class and of all the people. The working class had to take the lead in overcoming capitalism since changes in the mode of production would be a crucial input into transforming the existing common culture; and for this Bauer believed a 'socialist federation of nationalities' would be required.

If Bauer also accepted that there were 'non-historic' peoples he did at least allow for them to be re-awakened by capitalism.

His emphasis on 'cultural-national autonomy' with its implied recognition of the equality of all cultures was certainly welcome but the main problem with the Austro-Marxists was that the political perspective they offered was quite inadequate for their times. In the context of the existing Tsarist Empire, Bauer called for civil equality and federation within the Empire rather than calling for the overthrow of Tsarist rule. This had organizational implications. In contrast to Lenin's effort to build a more centralized party structure as a fighting instrument (whether operating underground or openly) Bauer's perspective called for a federated structure much more loosely bound since overthrowing the Tsarist state was not supposed to be on the current agenda. Nor was cultural-national autonomy a substitute for the much more democratic call for respecting the 'right to self-determination' that Lenin would put forward.

Luxemburg and Lenin

Even though Rosa Luxemburg opposed national oppression she rejected the idea that there could be the 'right to self-determination'. Like Bauer she preferred to endorse autonomy and federalism. She denied that nations or peoples can have the right to self-determination believing that this would play into the hands of the ruling class. Moreover, like most classical Marxists she thought small nations would be unviable and in any case promoting national unity and nation-state formation belonged to the era of the rising bourgeoisie, not now. For Lenin the national state was the norm under capitalism and such states could be big or small. He also preferred big units but recognized that these should come about voluntarily and believed that smaller nations would eventually integrate either as a consequence of capitalist compulsions or through socialist internationalism. The multinational state under capitalism (like Tsarist Russia) would be backward or reactionary but even here he allowed for an exception–Greater Austria which was stable and capitalist though encompassing Germans, Hungarians and Slavs. Luxemburg believing that in many cases the struggle for national independence was a diversion from class struggle would assign the 'right to self-determination' only to the working class not to the 'people' as a whole. Furthermore, she believed there could be no such thing as absolute rights since rights were always contextual. So certainly support freedom from oppression—national or otherwise—but what sense did it make to say there is a 'right' to freedom from oppression.[41]

Later Marxists including Lenin had to address nationalist upsurges in Eastern Europe, Tsarist Russia and anti-colonial struggles. Lenin was not looking to develop any theory of nationalism but seeking a practical political perspective and guideline for advancing the socialist cause which he believed also meant advancing democracy since there could in his eyes be no contradiction between the two.[42] If in Western Europe he saw the 'national question' as settled, this was not so in Persia, Turkey, Russia, China and the Balkans where bourgeois democratic national movements had emerged. Lenin also for the first time took up the colonial question and allied national liberation movements, where they were developing, to the socialist cause. After 1914 and the outbreak of inter-imperialist wars he saw these anti-imperialist struggles along with class struggles as central to socialist internationalism.

From his writings after 1914 we can see the evolution of his thinking and to this day (though it is by no means a magic wand to be waved in all cases) his formulae—for respecting the 'right to self-determination' of an oppressed nation or nationality; for the stands to be taken by revolutionaries in the oppressor and oppressed nations; for prioritizing the interests of proletarian internationalism—remain amongst the most important and treasured legacies of the socialist tradition for dealing with the 'national question' itself extended in what it is meant to refer to, and cover.[43] Lenin's key points were as follows: (i) distinguish between the interests of oppressed classes and the notion of 'national interests'. (ii) Distinguish between 'oppressed, dependent and subject nations and the oppressing, exploiting and sovereign nations.'[44] (iii) Communist parties must aid revolutionary movements among dependent and 'underprivileged nations' (American blacks—then referred to as Negroes—were seen as an underprivileged nation), and in the colonies. (iv) Proletarian struggle within a country should be subordinated to the interests of the proletarian struggle internationally.[45] (v) On the colonial question Lenin's views were modulated by the influence of M.N. Roy's warnings about the duplicities of the indigenous bourgeoisie which could well collaborate with the imperialist bourgeoisie against the revolutionary classes. So Lenin, while arguing that Communist parties should have a temporary alliance with the bourgeois-led national liberation movement, made this conditional on being able to retain its organizational independence and having the freedom to propagate its ideology. (vi) Lenin emphasized the danger of, and therefore opposition to, big nation chauvinism vis-à-vis smaller and weaker nationalities. Indeed, true equality among nationalities to be more than just formal, would require the big nation to have greater sensitivity and to 'bend over backwards' in unequally giving favours without return to smaller nations/nationalities.

Three guiding principles thereby emerged. There should be a unity of the working class across all nations. Recognize the equality of all nations and cultures so an important degree of autonomy within a state, is required.[46] It is necessary to raise the slogan of respecting the 'right to self-determination' provided there was a national movement taking place among that nation/nationality which was also an oppressed one. After Lenin, what Marxists had called the National Question that now needed to be resolved in a just manner that would advance the democratic and socialist cause, was extended beyond the issue of national unity and consolidation for capitalist functionality to (a) the legitimacy or otherwise of annexations by one state of another; (b) dealing with the issue of secessionist pressures; (c) matters concerning national minorities within a state; (d) matters regarding support to anti-colonial struggles.

On the issue of supporting the right to self-determination up to and including secession, two normative questions arise. Should a minority community wishing to be politically distinct from a majority community have the democratic right to do so? Are nationalist forms of autonomy or separation politically desirable? Liberals would use as their guideline the principle that the 'right has priority over the good'. Liberal Communitarians and

Republicans, Marxists and Anarchists believing in the need for establishing a 'common and collective good' would more strongly emphasize the importance of the latter. Without addressing the normative issues directly, Lenin's formula is still the best thing going politically, seeking to respect and combine the pursuit of both the right and the good. A socialist inspired territorial unity in which the working classes and revolutionaries of both the oppressor and oppressed nations come together to overthrow the state rule of their common oppressors would be ideal, but any such territorial unity must be *voluntary*. Revolutionaries in the oppressor nationality must therefore criticize that national oppression and uphold the banner of respecting the right to self-determination for the oppressed nationality; while revolutionaries in the oppressed nationality should emphasize the value of a collective and united socialist struggle to overthrow common class oppressors. One side emphasizes the 'right to secede', the other side the 'right to unite'. This remains the best political way to deal with the tension between democratic right and common good.

Stalin and the Subsequent Soviet Experience[47]

One year before Lenin's 1914 article on 'The Right to Self-Determination', Stalin had written his 'Marxism and the National Question' which had been unduly praised by many including Lenin, thereby giving it a status it didn't deserve. In this tract Stalin presented a strict objective definition of the nation or nationality which would create more problems than solutions. For Stalin a 'nation is a historically constituted, stable community of people formed on the basis of a common language, territory, economic life and psychological make-up manifested in a common culture'.[48] So, multi-lingual entities were not to be seen as nations. Switzerland was a state not a nation. Going by Stalin's definition a national minority was a non-nation which could not grow into becoming a nation and would be assimilated by the process of capitalist internationalization. He talked of national minorities or non-nations being absorbed in the 'melting pot' of the host nationality. National cultural autonomy was not something to admire or endorse. Only later did Stalin come around to accepting that such minorities could get partial autonomy. Similarly, though in his tract he made no distinction between oppressor and oppressed nationalities he would come around later to a formal acceptance of Lenin's distinction, though in letter and spirit as his subsequent record would show, he diverged fundamentally from the perspectives Lenin held.[49]

In 1913 Lenin had argued for a centralized socialist regime but by 1918 he came to accept the principle of national republics. 'The Soviet Russian Republic is established on the basis of a free union of free nations as a federation of Soviet national republics.'[50] In fact, the Russian Revolution of 1917 was remarkable not just for being the first 'revolution against capital' but it was also a 'revolution against the order of nations'. To this day, the only country whose very name bore no reference to a people or a territory was that of the USSR–the Union of Soviet Socialist Republics! Insofar as the Soviet Constitution would carry this commitment to Lenin's self-determination principle, this was both a time-bomb and a pragmatic way of maintaining cohesion. Everything would of course depend on actual Soviet practice.[51] That experience turned out to be very mixed.

The democratic revolution of February 1917 caused a considerable disintegration of the Empire and an upsurge in nationalist movements in the border areas. After the October revolution of 1917 and in the following year, the independence of Finland and of the Baltic Republics of Latvia, Lithuania and Estonia were recognized and accepted.[52] Non-Russian peoples in the Tsarist periphery were generally sympathetic to the Bolshevik government. But Georgia, Armenia and Ukraine had national movements which required careful handling (in Ukraine public influence was divided between the larger nationalists and the Ukraine Communists), elsewhere absent such movements, autonomy rather than separation was on the agenda. How the Bolsheviks would handle the situation would decide the balance between persuasion and force in establishing the Soviet Union. Thus in the Central Asian republics early and promising prospects of working with

Muslim communists led by Sultan Galiev who wanted to establish a larger Muslim-dominated republic within the USSR motivated partly by his concern about Great Russian chauvinism, foundered on the rocks of mutual distrust between himself and Stalin and other Bolshevik leaders. He fell prey to Stalin's purge in 1928, being sentenced to death, then exiled, then arrested again in 1937 and finally shot in 1940.

The fact is that the establishment of the USSR was not based only on voluntary union. Force was also used in many cases often as a short-cut rather than working patiently to win over local populations to the merits of a unity that would also respect the principle of an internal equality between all nationalities which above all meant ensuring that there would be no excuse for any complaints about Great Russian chauvinism. Lenin's last battles against Stalin and others who supported him within the party was precisely his anger at such chauvinist behaviour and centralizing excesses in the cases of Ukraine and Georgia. Certainly there was a qualitative difference between Lenin and Stalin in their respective understandings of the national question, their political sensitivities and therefore in their policy perspectives and behaviour. But even for Lenin there was a fundamental dilemma he could not overcome. He had thought that there would be no serious tension or contradiction between the pursuit of socialist unity (all the more necessary in a context where internal and external forces had sought to crush the new Soviet regime) and the defence of democratic rights and principles. But there was this tension! And it pushed the Bolshevik leadership as a whole to prioritize the principle of unity. The 'right to unite' would increasingly override the 'right to secede'.

Under Stalin's rule, 15 Union Republics were established that were nominally equal but much greater power was given to the federal government to ensure a centralized structure of power. Some 16 'autonomous republics', 9 'autonomous regions' and 10 'autonomous units' were established. Great Russians made up 55 per cent of the population, Ukrainians were 18 per cent and Byelorussians were 4 per cent—all Eastern Slavs. Given the weight of Russians in the overall population it is not surprising that Stalin would push a 'Great Russian Patriotism' to act as some kind of social glue even rehabilitating Ivan the Terrible and glorifying an older history of Russian expansionism. In his great purge of 1937-38, Stalin liquidated in part or whole the governments of 30 republics for 'national deviation', while in the Second World War he exiled whole populations–Crimean Tartars, Volga Germans, Kalmyks, Chechens and other Caucasian peoples for fear of their possible disloyalty to Russian dominated Moscow.[53] Yet these contingent acts were one part of the bigger story.

Article 17 of the Soviet Constitution gave the right to secede to every Union Republic but final decision would still lie in the hands of the Communist Party of the Soviet Union (CPSU) which itself was monolithic with no 'national federated' and 'autonomous' units. But proportionality in filling up local party and administrative positions was seriously pursued. Thus a 'whole stratum was built up of minor officials who had a stake in the regime.....'[54] Stalin's rule also promoted ethnic and national consciousness in the non-Russian republics through recognizing cultures and languages. Though there was a disproportionate influence of Russians at the centre this was meliorated by propping up non-Russian elites whose access to power relied not just on their alignment to this centre but in their being seen as genuine representatives of specific ethnicities. So during Stalin's time and in the post-war decades after, ethnic identity ironically, was made more important than class identity while the ruling bureaucracy and the *Nomenklatura* were made more stable for being ethnically diversified. If the flow of resources from the centre to the non-Russian republics further helped to stabilize the rule of the Communist party throughout the USSR, it is also true that in civil society in the various republics, a nationalist rather than socialist idiom would become more dominant.[55]

With the arrival of Gorbachev's *glasnost* or democratization efforts, nationalist stirrings would grow in some cases e.g. in the Baltic Republics and to a lesser extent in Georgia and Armenia with Ukraine a further laggard. But most others would have preferred to stay together in a more truncated Union if a genuine federalism could emerge with restored rights for the smaller oppressed minorities such Tartars, Ingush, Chechens, Kalmyks, etc. *Perestroika's* shift to marketization worsened matters economically for the majority of people, creating stronger centrifugal pressures for a more substantial break-up than might otherwise have taken place.[56] However, to make the nationalities issue central to explaining the break-up of the Soviet Union would be a serious error. This was more the result of the break-up than the cause. Despite growing disillusionment with the Soviet experiment because of the democratic unhappiness with one-party rule and the widespread public sense of economic failures associated with the top-down command system of organizing development, no previous 'empire' ever collapsed so quickly, so comprehensively, and, relatively speaking, with so little bloodshed–only around 3,000 died. The USSR had covered one-third of the world's surface, had 300 million people and contained some forty significant nationalities or national minorities. It was not rebellion from below but disillusionment at the top that paved the way for the break-up. Those who most benefited from the earlier system had themselves lost hope and belief in the system and thought to better advance their own interests through a break-up. Boris Yeltsin's own ambitions and the role he played in discarding any effort to retain even a truncated USSR rather than a Russian Federation of which he would be the first President, was basically a reflection of the wider and deeper inter-play of power between Russian nationalists out to secure their rule at the expense of the conservative old-timer Communists of the former Soviet *Nomenklatura*.

Today's World: Capitalism and the Nation-State System

Historically, Marxists were among those who believed that the nation-state would soon enough turn out to be an anachronism buffeted by two forces, first by capitalist expansionism, and then by the advance of the socialist revolution. Worldwide developments since the late 1970s have forced a re-evaluation of this early optimism more so with regard to the prospects of socialism, partially so with respect to the issue of nationalism. If future prospects for the nation-state system are considered to be not that bright, responsibility for this is now sought to be laid at the door of capitalism in its latest phase of 'globalization' and with the growing power and importance of transnational corporations (TNCs) as economic actors. In some sections of the Left this has given rise to talk of both the decline of the nation-state and the emergence of a 'transnational capitalist class.'[57]

This is not the perspective upheld here. In fact, in the very period when global movements of capital, money, goods and services has become greater than ever before while movement of labour across borders has also been considerable, the number of nation-states has actually increased. This reality could be dismissed as the contingent result of the break-ups of the former USSR and Yugoslavia but elsewhere in one or other part of the world there continue to be nationalist tensions carrying popular aspirations to possible separate nationhood in Spain (Basque region and Catalonia), UK (Scotland and the Irish question), Canada (Quebec), South Asia (Kashmir), the Middle East (Palestine and Kurdistan), Republic of Cameroon in West Africa, China (Xinjiang and Taiwan), Russia (Chechnya) while the Republic of South Sudan and Kosovo are recent newcomers to the comity of nations. There are, in short, no signs that might justify prognostications of the steady decay in the medium, let alone short term of the nation-state system. The question raised on the Left then, is whether we need to assess once more, the nature of the relationship between the capitalism of our times and the nation-state system.[58]

Since for Marxists the *nation*-state (not the state in general) owes its emergence to the rise of capitalist modernity what reason is there to think that the nation-state will disappear short of the disappearance of capitalism? Indeed, the trans-nationalization of social relations and the consolidation and juridical sharpening of territorialized sovereignty went together.[59] For the foreseeable future we will see both the continuing logic of capitalist accumulation on a world scale and a multiple nation-states system. The two have now coexisted and connected for a sufficiently long period of time that we must accept that there exists a strong functional relationship between capitalism and the nation-states system. But how powerful a factor is this in maintaining this 'duality within a totality'? Since capitalism was born in an already existing multiple states system, could this multiplicity have imposed its logic on capitalism and therefore been a key factor in securing the contemporary order?

One view is that had capitalism been born in a context where there existed a world empire there is no reason to think that the logic of capitalist accumulation would have required a territorial break-up of this 'inheritance'. That is to say, capitalist competition or the fact of 'many capitals' does not promote, nor in itself require that there be 'many states'. There is no strong functionalism between the two contemporary realities.[60] More persuasive is the contrasting view of those who insist on an important functionalism and also on the fact that the separation of the economic and political in the capitalist mode of production does create a practical dynamic in favour of there being many states which (for reasons already enunciated in the first part of this text) are nation states legitimized in the name of nationalism.[61] Capitalism's intrinsic nature only requires trans-nationalization of economic relations plus a mechanism for global stabilization for capital accumulation which can be provided in flexible ways in a capitalist inter-state system. Moreover, the separation of the economic and political creates a 'privatized' sphere of surplus value accumulation and extraction, and another sphere of the exercise of political power by a 'public' authority. There are now capitalists and state managers, each having different functions, interests and motivations. Given this separation of functions, capitalists do not have the time, compulsion or interest in organizing the political terrain even at the level of the domestic, let alone at the international level. Competition between capitalists means the class as a whole cannot be the governing category. In fact, the capitalist ruling class is the first such class that does not itself rule![62]

This governing group (state managers) of course must be connected to and structurally biased towards capitalists and capitalism but must also supply mechanisms for cooperation between capitals, provide rules and norms for stable competition, and arbitrate in intra-capitalist conflicts. This is the first of the internal functions of the state. The second is that the state must control class conflict in favour of the capitalist class as a whole which may well require it from time to time to act against this or that section of capitalists depending on the strength of resistance from below. A third function is the role of the state in dealing with crisis situations both economic (through Keynesian-type measures and bailouts of those firms that are 'too big to fail' as in the recent 2007/8-2012 Great Recession) and socio-political.

Then there is the external function. All capitals benefit from an expansion of space in which they can operate to secure more profits. But the world is too large a space to ensure the broad regularity and predictability that capital needs for its dynamic and constant pursuit of expanded reproduction. Furthermore, competition between capitals on this expanded scale means there will always be losers as well as winners and the former, especially when they are sizeable TNCs, will not simply sit back and quietly accept this.[63] They often look for and get 'protection' from their home state. Nor is it a surprise that the shifting geography of the competition for surplus value will often bring into play 'conflicts of interests' between states themselves.

Intrinsic to capital is the principle of competition. The market is supposed to embody the principle of coordination–the broom of efficiency–that determines the distribution of success and failure. However, these very market operations also cause tensions and instabilities between capitals which to some degree or the other do transmute into tensions between states; tensions which are quite separate from and in addition to other historically constituted geo-political problems that may exist among states. But the principle that is external to both capital and the market and yet is necessary for capital to function properly is the mechanism for providing global stabilization. If the individual nation-state seeks to provide this stability at the domestic level, and the nation-states system to try and do the same at the global level, who or what will stabilize the nation-states system?

This is where thought-frames within Marxism and within the Liberal Realist tradition of thinking on international relations tend to converge. If the latter will talk of the 'international public good' that is provided by 'hegemonic stability', the former will point to a sub-set of the most powerful imperialist powers who must take up this stabilizing role to guarantee the continuity of capitalist exploitation and oppression on a world scale. And does this sub-set itself need a key coordinator-stabilizer to handle tensions within? Here is where there is again something of a Marxist replay of the issue whether we should nonetheless be highlighting the importance of a single hegemon; or can this stabilization, in our current post-Communist times, become the shared responsibility of a small collective of Great Powers, all capitalist? This is where the questions concerning the status of US power, relative and absolute, come centre-stage. Could the establishment of this current phase of neoliberal capitalist globalization that emerged from the late 1970s onwards have even taken place without the crucial exercise of American power at various levels? What will happen now with the rise of China and other emergent or emerging capitalist powers? Can there be a substitute, single or collective, for the global role hitherto played by the US? What are the implications of failure in this regard? How will the future 'dialectic between the national and the international' unfold?[64]

These are large questions that cannot be addressed here. But there is an additional argument provided for why a multiple states system has so far endured. This has to do with the character of the state rather than with capitalism. Simon Bromley says that while mainstream International Relations focuses on the consequences of a multiple inter-state system, and Marxists on the relationship between the states system and societies (capitalist or otherwise). But neither says Bromley, pay proper attention to the issue of politics and the *political order* where the question of the 'use of force' comes in.[65] *Politics can be understood as that dimension of the social life concerned with arriving at and giving effect to collectively binding decisions and rules.* People are social beings whose agency can be erased by force, hence the need for individual and collective security which has to be a key aspect of installing public order. For there to be such order there have to be rules and institutions but given conflicts of interest between individuals and groups, the possibility of coercion exercised by a public authority is unavoidable. But while there are different forms of coercion that can restrict or curtail the free exercise of agency, force is still different from coercion in that it attacks agency itself.[66] For the exercise of force there has to be what Bromley calls 'physical co-presence' which in turn requires 'territorial proximity.' Political order then for him can only be for a segment of the human population and for a segment of the planet's territorial space. Political life means there will be 'insiders' and 'outsiders'. Or as Bromley puts it, 'We live together politically if we live under a political order at all, in a qualitatively different way to the ways in which we might live together economically or culturally. The corollary of this is that we also live *apart* politically in ways that are different to our economic and cultural differences.'[67]

The transcendence of capitalism on a world scale may or may not eradicate an inter-state system completely. But it is only conceivable on the basis of a much deeper and widespread understanding and acceptance of an internationalism that by its very nature replaces the pull of nationalism even if for part of the journey an increasingly progressive internationalism will have to go along with the pursuit of more progressive nationalisms. But given that we are now faced for the first time in human history with three great and universal evils that are intimately connected to a globalizing capitalism, the need for transcending it should be deemed incontestable. The human species itself is threatened by possible mass devastation through dangers humanly created. Now more than ever is there a need for a response that subordinates our national differences to what we collectively share as global dilemmas. (1) Even as there is the most obscene and historically unmatched levels of wealth concentration and inequality, 'Basic Needs' (which now go well beyond the eradication of malnutrition to include health, education, leisure, respect and personal dignity, freedom from fear) for so much of the world's population are and will remain unmet. This is not because of scarcity of resources but in spite of the fact that for some time now the age of such scarcity *globally* is finally over! (2) Ecological limits of various kinds are in the process of being crossed with profound negative consequences for the delicate metabolism that connects humans with nature. (3) The cloud of a nuclear conflagration and nuclear winter looms constantly over us even as it shifts its geographical positioning.

The Imperialism of Human Rights

In the post-Cold War era it bears reminding ourselves that in contrast to the sacralised and personalized states of the pre-modern past the advent of nationalism and of the nation-state was an important democratic advance because of the principle inherent in it of popular sovereignty i.e. rule in the name of the collective interest of the 'people' constituted as the nation. Moreover, if one were asked to identify what on the world scale constituted the *single greatest democratic advance* in the second half of the twentieth century the answer should be both obvious and incontestable. It was decolonization, even where a local dictatorship replaced foreign colonial rule. One of the crucial background conditions, objectively speaking, that greatly facilitated rapid decolonization was the presence of a socialist bloc of countries that supported decolonization and in opposition to Western powers provided (however selective and half-hearted at times) material and political-diplomatic support to anti-colonial movements and struggles, and vied with the West for influence in these newly independent countries. The legal-political reflection of the reality of decolonization at the international level was the institutionalization of the principle of formal equality and national self-determination of all nation-states. Thus the supremacy of state sovereignty was declared in Article 2(1) in the UN Charter; that of non-interference and the ban on armed force from outside is embodied in Article 2(7) of the UN Charter with the only exception allowed being the 'right to self-defence' in Article 2(4) of the same Charter. Chapter VII of the Charter says that if a state threatens a 'breach of international peace' then as a last resort measure (when all other steps have been tried and failed) armed action can be sanctioned by the Security Council (SC) against that state.[68]

It is not a coincidence that with the collapse of the socialist bloc of countries, the UN has been much more easily suborned by the US and that external military intervention in the name of 'humanitarian intervention' and 'regime change in the name of democracy' became the new ideological banners in which the West led by the US dramatically escalated their selective interventions in the developing world. Selective in that this is not directed against allies no matter how authoritarian they are or when they carry out a 'breach of the international peace' by their illegal military acts e.g. those by Israel over the years both inside and outside the Occupied Territories, and by Saudi Arabia more recently in Bahrain and Yemen.[69] This has rightly been called the 'imperialism of human rights' and is invariably justified in the name of national interest(s) by the external intervening power(s). Never absent though are claims about the more universal or international political-cum-normative virtues of taking such a course. It is this political-cum-normative claim that needs to be investigated here.

The issue is not external intervention *per se* but about *forcible* i.e. military intervention for humanitarian reasons which is a category of action qualitatively distinct from the application of international sanctions against the government in question and even from external supply of arms to a particular combatant in an internal civil war situation. There are three stances or positions one can take. The first is to rule out all and any exceptions to what is already laid down in international law and the UN Charter. The five main arguments, for why there should be an unqualified rejection of any such military intervention taking place, are as follows. (1) Do not ignore the issue of the motives of the intervener(s). States don't intervene for humanitarian but for politically self-interested reasons and purposes. (2) State sovereignty is supreme. Citizens are the exclusive responsibility of their state and their state is entirely their business. (3) Don't promote the further possibility and likelihood of abuse by adding another 'exception' in the name of human rights to what already exists by way of exception in the UN Charter. (4) There will always be selective application of the principle of forcible humanitarian intervention. Therefore, there will always be inconsistency in this policy. (5) There is no agreed consensus among the states of the world on what should be the principles on which forcible humanitarian intervention would be justified. It is better for the world that the order, currently provided by upholding the principle of non-intervention that already legally exists (and is near universally accepted), be re-affirmed than to allow the internal disorder that would result from accepting periodic violations of this principle in the name of human rights.

The second stance is to insist on forcible humanitarian intervention; and here the basic arguments are as follows. (1) Promotion of human rights is at least as important, if not more so, than international peace and security. Articles 1(3), 55 and 56 of the UN are, or should be, as or more important than the exception provided by 2(4).[70] (2) Legally these articles cannot be said to override the existing injunctions concerning external military intervention. But it is argued that whatever the legal position this is not the same as the moral position. Morality may require in certain cases forcible humanitarian intervention to end slaughter. The existence of a legal right *enables* action but does not *determine* it. (3) It is outcomes not motives that are paramount. Also outcomes are both short-term/immediate and longer-term. The short-term considerations are met by intervention to stop the human suffering. But there are also longer-term considerations to be met so intervention can and should in certain cases be prolonged to ensure proper economic, social, political reconstruction. How long will be the period of 'prolonged' intervention, will of course be decided by the intervener.[71]

There is a third 'qualified intervention' position to which I subscribe. This is closer to the first than to the second stance. It states that for the most part forcible humanitarian intervention is not justified because one must respect the right of a people to overthrow their own tyrant. That is to say, the suffering people must themselves be seen as the primary agency of their own future. This is a normative stance of respecting a collective's 'freedom of agency' which cannot be substituted for by an external agency. So a colonial oppressor and the end of colonial rule must be carried out by the colonized themselves with whatever help (including military) from outside; but it cannot be delivered by an external military intervention. The same applied to the case of the South African apartheid regime and, for another example, the overthrow of the Shah of Iran. The only qualifications to this principle when one would support an external forcible intervention is first when one side in a domestic conflict or civil war situation calls for, and gets, external military intervention on its side. Then the other side could be justified in calling and getting the same. This is what happened in southern Africa in the cases of Angola and Namibia in the 1970s/80s when South African forces under an apartheid government intervened and were countered and defeated by invited Cuban troops.

The second case would be when the situation is so grave that the very existence of a 'people' in substantial part or whole is threatened. Here outcomes not motives do become more important. After all, respect for the right of a people to overthrow their own tyrant must presume the existence of the people. Ethnic cleansing i.e. expulsion but not massacre of a very substantial section of the population would not justify forcible intervention for they still exist. There is, however, an unavoidable ambiguity in this respect. There can be no definitive answer to the question of how large-scale a massacre would have to take place or is likely to take place, in order for one to arrive at a judgement that a people's existence is being threatened and therefore the necessity of carrying out an immediate intervention since this judgement is also connected to the absolute size of the overall population. Thus, on one hand, the massacre of around 500,000 civilians during Bangladesh's war of liberation–given the overall size of the population and the fact that the Mukti Bahini actually fighting the armed struggle within Bangladesh (for all their appreciation of Indian material support) were adamant that liberation should be the task of Bangladeshis themselves–would not have justified India's military intervention.[72] On the other hand, the massacre by Indonesia of 300,000 or one-third of East Timor's population would have justified an external humanitarian intervention to stop this but did not get it. A similar case was that of Rwanda in 1994 when some 800,000 or 70 per cent of Tutsis in the country were being slaughtered over a 100 day period. What made matters even more shocking was that while Romeo Dallaire, the then head of the UN peacekeeping forces already posted there, was pleading to the Security Council for more military support, the US acted to discourage a robust UN support until too late.

The UN definition of genocide is of no help since it talks of not just the whole of a population being threatened but also of an unspecified 'part' of the population and therefore lends itself to labelling even small-scale killings as genocide. The claim of genocide having taken place was then unjustifiably used to endorse NATO intervention in the Balkan conflicts after the collapse of Yugoslavia. By this third standard of 'qualified intervention' where external military interventions by any force or concert of powers whether UN sponsored or not, should have taken place, these did not happen. Here the examples of East Timor in 1975 and Rwanda in 1994 stand out. A necessary act of intervention that did take place, though the motive was not principally humanitarian but nevertheless deserved to be supported, was actually condemned by most Western democracies–namely, the intervention by Vietnam in Kampuchea to overthrow the Pol Pot regime which in proportionate terms outdid the horrific massacres carried out by Hitler of Jews, gypsies and other designated 'enemies' of the Third Reich.[73]

In the post-Cold War era, the masks of humanitarian and moral concern has been more frequently donned mainly but not solely by the West (one must not let off Russia, China and a host of 'emerging powers' that include the likes of India and Turkey) to cover their imperialist behaviour. This is all the more reason, then, to recognize and oppose the 'imperialism of human rights'!

Competing Nationalisms in India

Currently there is an ongoing battle for how one should understand Indian nationalism. The very fact that we have a BJP government in power, headed by a man with a hardcore Hindutva mind set, is a clear indication of the significant strides that have been already made by the Sangh Parivar to impose their vision of India and its nationalism. There are those on the Left who believe the era of the nation-state and therefore of the ideology they associate with it—namely nationalism—is basically coming to an end and it is the pursuit of global democratic governance that should be the priority. They differ from liberal cosmopolitans in that the sought for global order must not be capitalist. Given the problems (some of which have been highlighted earlier) that must now be tackled globally the terrain of anti-capitalist struggles must, they say, now be shifted to the extra-national and global terrains. Here, the basic orientation to nationalism is to see it as a basically negative phenomenon possessing little or no virtue. The global and the national are seen as *conflicting* principles of organization. Therefore, insofar as one will have to fight against the forces of Hindutva in India this should be done in the name of democracy and internationalism but not in the name of an alternative conception of nationalism to that being promoted by the Sangh Parivar.

However, for reasons that have to do with the continued importance of the nation-states system for capitalism, whether operating within or across countries, and because of nationalism's powerful appeal to popular loyalties, we cannot escape political engagement at the level of the national. Marx, who in his *Manifesto* showed that he was really the first theorist of globalization (though not of imperialism) nevertheless also recognized that the working class to eradicate capitalism worldwide, would still first have to settle accounts with it at many a national level. The struggle for generating a progressive internationalism will require struggles to promote progressive changes at the national level as well. In India, given the determination of the forces of Hindutva, to define the meaning of nationalism in the way they want means that they have to be confronted with a very different understanding of nationalism. That is to say, a nationalist vision that is much more open and inclusive and therefore constructed through wider struggles for democracy and radical transformation. But such a *national* project must also recognize its limits and its subordination to the even wider project of progressive global transformation.

In one of his numerous writings the late Benedict Anderson suggested that nationalism can be seen in two ways. It can be seen as something belonging to the past, an inheritance of some sort. In which case there is likely to be endless disputes about what the proper inheritance is and who are the proper inheritors? In India two competing versions of this 'cultural nationalism' (as the supposed essence of Indian political nationalism) are the respective historical legacies of 'Hindu religion and culture' (described in variant ways) and the notion of a 'composite culture' to which many plural cultural and religious currents are said to have contributed. But the latter is not a serious counter to the former. For the question then arises of what particular ingredient plays the biggest role in helping to 'compose' this plural cultural admixture, that is supposed to lie at the heart of Indian nationalism? And here the candidate for the status as key composer that gets the most applause from various circles including those perceiving themselves as highly secular, is Hinduism. Moreover, both perspectives subscribe to the myth that a unique characteristic of India through the ages that has shaped its nationalism is its socio-culture *tolerance*. Here cultural plurality, coexistence, and diversity are being misread as meaning tolerance. However, any modern, as distinguished from any pre-modern, notion of tolerance is umbilically tied to a political culture of rights, individual and collective, which itself is a post-Enlightenment, modern development. No equivalent 'culture of rights' as ever existed anywhere in the past.

This 'inheritance' approach to nationalism in the hands of Hindutva acolytes insists on there being a cultural essence–in this case 'Hinduness' as interpreted by them–which must then be recognized, appreciated and strengthened. For it is on this foundation of 'cultural strength' that a strong nation can be erected. And for this the unity of Hindus is paramount. Furthermore, as Savarkar sloganized during the Second World War, 'Hinduize all politics and militarize Hindudom'.[74] But one can try and unite Hindus in only two ways. One way is to try and find a principle of ideological unity internal to Hinduism and organize around that. The only possible candidate for this is a loose and accommodating

Brahminism. But given the cultural-emotional-material ballasts that Brahminism provides to the caste system, one can only go so far in this desired unification process. Greater prospects of success in this project of creating Hindu unity are deemed to come from finding and then organizing around a principle of unification that is external to Hinduism, i.e. to postulate a 'common enemy for *all* Hindus'. Here the 'best' candidate for villainy, given the Hindutva construction of Indian history, is Muslims and Islam.

Thus the political project of Hindutva is by its very nature anti-secular, anti-democratic and viciously communal. The *cultivation of deliberately constructed grievances* so as to arouse collective Hindu anger, fear and even hatred then requires militant and aggressive posturing and mobilizing around (a) presumed iniquities of the historical past requiring rectification, symbolic or otherwise e.g. the Babri-Masjid-Ram Janmabhoomi issue; (b) contemporary issues of presumed 'bias/partiality/favouritism' by the state e.g. Article 370 or Muslim Personal Law; (c) presumed threats to the existence of the Hindu family and ways of life e.g. 'love jihads' by young Muslim males; (d) mortal dangers represented by Indian Muslims who are guilty by virtue of mere religious identity of sympathy for or association with Pakistan-based terrorists, and are constituted as an actual or potential fifth column for them, and the Pakistan state.[75]

Minority communalist politics and projects are morally speaking, equally reprehensible and must be opposed and fought against. But one must be clear that majority communalism is always more dangerous. One does not merely have in mind the disproportion in terms of deaths and casualties caused in communal riots by whoever are responsible–the overwhelming majority of riot victims throughout the history of communal outbreaks in India since independence are Muslims. But it must be understood that the ultimate political logic of minority communalisms is a movement towards separate nationhood while only majority communalism can hope to disguise itself as a form of nationalism and by doing so help to transform Indian society *as a whole* in a much more authoritarian fashion. Given the feedback relationships between all communalism, they all have to be fought against concurrently and with maximum vigour. But the distinctive and more powerful danger represented by Hindu communalism in India must never be minimized.

The second way of understanding nationalism is to see it as an ongoing political project that belongs to the present and future. That is to say, nationalism is what we will make of it! And in a multilingual, multi-religious, multi-ethnic society like India, that nationalism must not only be secular but democratic; where secularism is the necessary but not sufficient condition for having a democratic state. So more important than Indian nationalism being secular it has to be democratic. And this means that all the citizens of the country should be able to feel a loyalty to that country and state that is not coerced but freely given. Not, as pointed out earlier, a nationalism that is constructed by supposed descent but by *consent* willingly given. That is to say, there must be *different ways* (and not one uniform or laid down or 'essential' way) of being and feeling Indian! This in turn is only possible if all the diverse communities that make up India feel that their respective cultures, languages, religions, etc. are respected; and that their secular needs and interests (as individuals and groups) are addressed with impartiality and fairness. This is why the construction of a more secular and democratic understanding of nationhood is crucial.

Nor can this process be separated from the larger issue of carrying out a wider transformation of the Indian polity, economy and society. Moreover, Marxists (and not only them) must reject that widespread understanding of nationalism as meaning or demanding loyalty to the nation above all else. The creation of the conditions for human flourishing is by its nature a universal and crosses all territorial borders. This has always been the lodestar guiding the allegiance to the socialist project. At a time when, as pointed out earlier, we are faced with dangers of a new kind caused by a globalizing capitalism to the human species itself, the classical socialist internationalism of agency (the international working class) and of its goals, remains paramount.

At the heart of this text then lies a simple enough, though difficult to achieve, injunction–that the pursuit of a capitalist transcending socialism on a world scale is now more necessary than ever before! Rosa Luxemburg had it right all along when she declared that the choice before us was 'Socialism or Barbarism'. And by barbarism she meant, not the collapse, but the continuity of capitalism itself!

Notes

1. Perennialist–Joshua Fishman, *Language and Nationalism: Two Integrative Essays*, Rowley, M.A., 1972. Primordialist–Steven Grosby, *Nationalism: A Very Short Introduction*, Oxford, 2005. Ethno-Symbolist–Anthony D. Smith, *Nationalism*, Oxford, 2001; and *Nationalism and Modernism: A Critical Survey of Recent Theories of Nations and Nationalisms*, London, 1998.
2. Organic nationalism sees the nation as an organism stamped by a fixed and indelible character because of some decisive cultural attribute that permanently marks its members by birth into that nation, for example, a unique German Volk spirit or the essential Hinduness of India. Philosophically, this understanding emerged really from the German Romantic tradition. According to this approach, nations are (a) natural entities; (b) each having a distinctive cultural essence; (c) of ancient origin; (d) the members of the nation may for various reasons lose consciousness of this uniqueness or have 'slumbered' for too long and need to be 're-awakened'; (e) the bonds binding the members are primordial and present for all even if in variable degrees of awareness and strength and these very bonds–formed by religion, language, custom, conventions, blood, extended kinship, common beliefs and values, etc. among all–is what makes that nation what it is.
3. Grosby, *Nationalism*, p. 14.
4. Ibid., p. 10.
5. Smith, *Nationalism and Modernism*, p. 6.
6. Bernard Yack, *Nationalism and the Moral Psychology of Community*, Chicago, 2012, pp. 69 and 91.
7. Zygmunt Bauman, *Mortality, Immortality and Other Life Strategies*, Oxford, 1992, p. 4.

8. Yack (*Nationalism and the Moral Psychology*) tries to defend the claim that the nation, like the ethnie, is above all a cultural entity of old, by separating the notion of the 'people' from the nation. The former is said to be connected to the state as a political entity while the nation need not be. So popular sovereignty or the 'people as being sovereign' is a modern development certainly, but is an attribute of the state only. Not only is this unconvincing in its own right, it cannot also help explain why even as a cultural entity, nationalism and national loyalty is so much more powerful (because of this political dimension) than other cultural group loyalties. Furthermore, Yack's cultural bias would make every multi-ethnic or poly-ethnic society e.g. the US, Australia, Canada and many European countries undergoing ethnic re-composition through migration, a multi-national society.
9. See Neil Davidson, *Nation-States, Consciousness and Competition*, Chicago, 2016, p. 4.
10. See Charles Taylor, 'Nationalism and Modernity' in Ronald Beiner (ed.), *Theorizing Nationalism*, New York, 1999.
11. John Breuilly, 'Reflections on Nationalism' in *Philosophy of the Social Sciences*, Vol. 15, 1985, pp. 74 and 75.
12. Eric J. Hobsbawm, *Nations and Nationalism Since 1780*, Cambridge, 1990. Hobsbawm, unlike Ben Anderson, did not wish to make the subjective dimension his starting point because of his unease with endorsing a voluntarism whereby if enough people in say, an island, want to form a nation they could. Nationalism which precedes the nation should be put under the microscope and anyway belonged to the era of the rising bourgeoisie. Nationalisms emerging in the last quarter of the 20th century were atavisms–the breakup of ex-USSR and of ex-Yugoslavia–were not welcomed by him as representing progressive advances. Hobsbawm never abandoned his critical loyalty but loyalty nonetheless to the Soviet Union nor did he ever come to proper terms with Stalinism and was insufficiently critical of the Soviet experience even with respect to the nationalities question. After the collapse of the USSR he gave up on the possibility of a capitalist transcending socialism, or in his words 'I am not surprised to find myself once again

among a generation that distrusts capitalism, though it no longer believes in our alternative to it.' E. Hobsbawm, *Interesting Times: A Twentieth-Century Life*, London, 2002, p. 414.

13. Tom Nairn, *Faces of Nationalism*, London, 1997.
14. Smith, *Nationalism and Modernism*, p. 5.
15. Elie Kedourie, *Nationalism*, London, 1960, and his *Nationalism in Asia and Africa*, London, 1971.
16. Breuilly, 'Approaches to Nationalism' in G. Balakrishnan (ed.), *Mapping the Nation*, London, 1996, p. 154. In a more recent piece (Breuilly, 'Nationalism as Global History' in Dapne Halikiopoulou and Sofia Vasilopoulou, *Nationalism and Globalisation: Conflicting or Complementary?* London, 2011) he argues that globalization came first then nationalism whose emergence was shaped by prior globalization. Given his view that nationalism is above all political, he naturally sees the spread of nationalism as taking place in five periods each having a distinct political character, namely the period of Anglo-French conflict 1750-1815; British hegemony 1815-1889; global imperial conflict 1880-1914; Cold War; Post-1990. For a very different and much more convincing characterization of the different *waves* of nation-state formation, see Benedict Anderson, *Imagined Communities*: *Reflections on the Origin and Spread of Nationalism*, London, 1991 where there is first the creole or settler nationalisms of the Americas, the linguistic nationalisms of Europe, then those following the break-up of the Austro-Hapsburg, Ottoman and Tsarist empires, then the anti-colonial nationalisms of the 'third world'. Moreover Anderson was prescient in suggesting that national rivalries between 'socialist regimes' could break the socialist bloc along nationalist lines.
17. Kai Nielsen, 'Cultural Nationalism, Neither Ethnic nor Civic' in Ronald Beiner (ed.), *Theorizing Nationalism*, New York, 1999, p. 127.
18. Benedict Anderson, *Imagined Communities*, London, 1991, p. 6.
19. If not in these words, this was nonetheless the gravamen of the argument put forward by Hans Kohn in his *The Idea of Nationalism*, New York, 1944, pp. 15-19. One need not and should not accept his distinction between 'good' liberal, civic, West European

nationalism and 'bad' illiberal, ethnic East European and Asian nationalism.

20. Liah Greenfeld, *The Spirit of Capitalism: Nationalism and Economic Growth*, Cambridge Mass. 2003 and her *Nationalism and the Mind*, Oxford, 2006.
21. Neil Davidson, *Nation-States: Consciousness and Competition*, Chicago, 2016.
22. See Charles Taylor, 'Nationalism and Modernity' in Ronald Beiner (ed.), *Theorizing Nationalism*, New York, 1999.
23. Taylor, 'Nationalism and Modernity", pp. 236 and 237.
24. Greenfeld, *The Spirit of Capitalism*, p. 24.
25. Greenfeld, *Nationalism and the Mind*, p. 94.
26. Ibid., p. 214.
27. Ibid., p. 213.
28. Ibid., p. 222.
29. Ibid., pp. 215 and 216. Also, see Taylor, the chapter on 'The Malaises of Modernity' in *A Secular Age*, 2007.
30. For a more detailed treatment of the issue of social order and its possible sources which is also critical of what can be called the 'cultural programming of society' see Achin Vanaik, *The Furies of Indian Communalism: Religion, Modernity, Secularization*, London, 1997 especially the sub-section on 'Culture and Society: The Problem of Order', pp. 82-94.
31. Mike Davis, 'Marx's Lost Theory' in *New Left Review II/93*, May-June 2015, p. 46.
32. See Gopal Balakrishnan, *Antagonistics*, London, 2009; pp. 170-176, where he says Anderson underestimates the importance of the fact that national preservation requires willingness and preparations for the possibility of war, making the nation a community of destiny or fate for its members who will be called upon when necessary for their ultimate self-sacrifice. Breuilly suggests that most theories of nationalism are too 'internalist' ignoring that globalization comes first, then nationalism; (see footnote 16). Actually, it is capitalism which promotes both globalization and nationalism but connecting nationalism to the transnational order

is necessary. Perry Anderson, the younger brother of Benedict, provides an acute survey of the changing forms of the couplet of nationalism-internationalism over seven phases of modern history, i.e. the last 275 years. See P. Anderson, 'Internationalism: A Breviary' in *New Left Review II/14*, March-April 2002.

33. See T.H. Aston and C.H.E. Philpin, *The Brenner Debate: Agrarian Class Structure and Economic Development in Pre-Industrial Europe*, Delhi, 2005 and Ellen Meiksens Wood, *The Origin of Capitalism: A Longer View*, London, 2002.
34. Davidson, *Nation-States*, Preface, p. xi.
35. Marx–'National differences and antagonisms between peoples are daily more and more vanishing......supremacy of the proletariat will cause them to vanish still further.' Marx and Engels, *Collected Works: 1845-48*, Vol. 6, London, 1976; p. 503. Engels–'The great mass of proletarians are, by their very nature, free from national prejudices....' Ibid., p. 6.
36. According to Roman Rosdolsky, this M and E view of historically immutable peoples was reflective of the continuing influence of Hegelian thinking where this German philosopher believed that world history progressed through a 'dialectic of several national minds' where some nations/nationalities which had already established powerful states had developed the necessary intellectual and spiritual capacities to progress as contrasted to other nations/ nationalities that were doomed to disappear. R. Rosdolsky, 'Engels and the Nonhistoric Peoples: The National Question in the Revolution of 1848' in *Critique 18-19*, 1986, p. 130.
37. Most Marxists of the past and present treat nation and nationality as synonymous terms. Classical Marxists of the past treated the nation or nationality as a culturally given entity abstracting from its political character. Of course in more recent times especially from the mid-20th century onwards, nationality has also developed a legal status and means that one is a citizen belonging to a particular state and therefore has the rights afforded by that state to its citizens. But nation and nationality are still treated as equivalent terms when it comes to identifying a distinct cultural-political entity.

38. To Lenin belongs the honour of decisively aligning the socialist cause to the anti-colonial cause.
39. See Mike Davis's, 'Marx's Lost Theory', 2015. This idea of the worker-peasant alliance being a revolutionary force if under working class leadership would later be taken up by Lenin in his pre-1917 argument for carrying out the bourgeois stage of revolution in Russia; and by Trotsky for carrying out the permanent revolution i.e. making the socialist revolution in Russia.
40. Bauer–'The nation is the totality of men bound together through a common destiny into a community of character.' See Ronaldo Munck, *The Difficult Dialogue: Marxism and Nationalism*, Delhi, 1986, p. 39.
41. Both with respect to nationalism and normative questions, later Marxists would learn from the Liberal tradition. There obviously are absolute or near-absolute rights because there are moral universals and there is moral learning across cultures and societies, e.g. no torture of children!
42. After the Russian Revolution when it came to the demands of some of the nationalities to self-determination Lenin behaved ambivalently and prioritized 'socialist unity' over democratic rights.
43. See his (a) 'The Right of Nations to Self-Determination', June 1914 in *Lenin: Selected Works*, Vol. 1, Moscow, 1975 (Revised); pp. 567-618. (b) 'Preliminary Draft Thesis on the National Question for Second Congress of the Communist International', June 14, 1920 in *Lenin: Selected Works*, Vol. 3, Moscow, 1975 (Revised), pp. 372-378. (c) 'Report of the Commission on the National and the Colonial Questions', August 7, 1920 in Ibid., pp. 405-409. (d) 'The Question of Nationalities or "Autonomization"', December 31, 1922 in Ibid., pp. 687-692.
44. *Lenin: Selected Works*, Vol. 3, p. 373.
45. Lenin was against pan-Islamism which he said, combined national liberation with promoting mullahs, landowners and other sections of the oppressing classes.
46. In practice this would mean non-discrimination and having vernacular schools and courts.

47. For two useful surveys of the differences between Lenin and Stalin, and of the post-1917 Soviet experience with regard to the nationalities question, see Horace B. Davis, *Toward a Marxist Theory of Nationalism*, New York/London, 1978, Chapters 3 and 4; and R. Munck, *The Difficult Dialogue*, Chapters 4 and 7.
48. Joseph Stalin, 'Marxism and the National Question'–Marxists Internet Archive; www.marxists.org/reference/archive/stalin/works/1913/03.htm
49. This would become evident in the clash between the two after the end of the civil war over the manner in which Ukraine and above all Georgia were being incorporated into the USSR. See "Last Testament" Letters to the Congress–Marxists Internet Archive www.marxists.org/archive/lenin/works/1922/dec/testament/
50. Munck, *The Difficult Dialogue*, p. 81.
51. Ronald Suny, 'Incomplete Revolution: National Movements and the Collapse of the Soviet Empire' in *New Left Review 189*, September-October 1991.
52. After the Hitler-Stalin Pact of 1939, these Baltic republics were forcibly brought into the fold of the USSR in 1940 and would remain so till the break-up of the Soviet Union in 1991 when they once again became independent countries.
53. Munck, *The Difficult Dialogue*, p. 127.
54. See Davis, *Towards a Marxist Theory of Nationalism*, pp. 91-92.
55. Suny, 'Incomplete Revolution'.
56. Ibid.
57. One of the foremost proponents of the emergence of a 'transnational capitalist class' (TCC) is William J. Robinson. See his *A Theory of Global Capitalism: Production, Class and State in a Transnational World*, Baltimore, 2004; 'Beyond the theory of imperialism: global capitalism and the transnational state' in Alexander Anievas (ed.) *Marxism and World Politics: Contesting Global Capitalism*, London/New York, 2010.
58. Two valuable surveys about the debate among Marxists on this score are Anievas, *Marxism and World Politics* and Chapter 7 on 'The Necessity of Multiple Nation-States for Capital' in Davidson, *Nation-States*, pp. 187-246.

59. The clearest exposition of this 'connected duality' appears in Justin Rosenberg, *The Empire of Civil Society: A Critique of the Realist Theory of International Relations*, London, 1994.
60. The foremost Marxist advocates for this view are Benno Teschke and Hannes Lacher. See their 'The changing "logic" of capitalist competition' in Anievas, *Marxism and World Politics*.
61. Reference has already been made in Section 1 on Nations and Nationalism about how, in the context of an historical decline in other kinds of social adhesives, nationalism has stepped in to try and provide psychic compensation, social cohesion, and to mobilize ground support for 'our' rulers against 'theirs'—a triple salve as it were.
62. Fred Block, 'The Ruling Class Does Not Rule: Notes on the Marxist Theory of the State' in his *Revising State Theory: Essays in Politics and Postindustrialization*, Philadelphia, 1987.
63. The overwhelming majority of today's TNCs are not multinational in their ownership patterns; and they generally have their key departments of financial and overall control and R& D located in their home rather than host countries.
64. See once again, Perry Anderson, "Internationalism: A Breviary', 2002.
65. Simon Bromley, 'Politics and the international' in Anievas, *Marxism and World Politics*.
66. Foucauldians ignore the fact that force is a special kind of power and therefore that the state is a very special and concentrated source of power because they don't sufficiently distinguish force from coercion.
67. Ibid., p. 234.
68. Achieving such a sanction from the SC does not automatically mean that military intervention is morally or politically justified. One of the five permanent members (most usually the US) can in pursuit of its national interest secure such a sanction for intervention through manipulation of SC voting members through use of the stick and carrot.
69. For a detailed account of the construction of post-Cold War ideological banners and the cover they have provided for Western intervention abroad, see Achin Vanaik (ed.), *Masks of Empire*, New

Delhi, 2007. The overarching ideological banner of the Cold War era under which Western powers justified their imperialist behaviour, was 'Protecting the Free World from the Communist Threat'. Soviet and Chinese expansionism was by contrast much less but also to be condemned. The new banners after the Collapse of Communism are (a) Humanitarian Intervention; (b) Regime Change in the Name of Democracy; (c) Global War on Terror; (d) WMDs in the 'Wrong Hands'; (e) Failed States; (f) War on Drugs. Each of these has been given separate chapter treatments. For how the UN itself has been suborned in various ways including introducing the new doctrine of 'Responsibility to Protect' see the chapter by Marianno Aguirre, 'Humanitarian Intervention and US Hegemony: A Reconceptualization'. See also the indictment of the general history of the UN's political system–the SC and UNGA–and of the record of Kofi Annan in particular, by Perry Anderson's, 'Our Man' in the *London Review of Books*, May 10, 2007.

70. The purposes of the UN as identified in Article 1(3) is 'To achieve international cooperation in solving international problems of an economic, social, cultural, or humanitarian character, and in promoting and encouraging respect for human rights and for fundamental freedoms for all without distinction as to race, sex, language, or religion.' Article 55–The UN shall promote 'universal respect for, and observance of, human rights and fundamental freedoms for all without distinction as to race, sex, language, or religion.' Article 56 is a supplement enjoining UN members to cooperate in securing the aims of Article 55.
71. Michael Walzer has argued for what he calls 'justice in endings' i.e. that a case can be made for an intervener to stay on after the war to ensure justice i.e. that there can and should be 'regime change in the name of democracy' even if the original intervention against an authoritarian regime e.g. as in Iraq in 2003 might be deemed unjustified. See, M. Walzer, 'the Aftermath of War' in Eric Patterson (ed.), *Ethics Beyond War's End*, Georgetown, 2012.
72. In this regard see the classic study by Lawrence Lifschultz, *Bangladesh: The Unfinished Revolution*, London 1979 which uncovers

the hidden stories of not just Pakistani but also of US and Indian machinations behind the scenes.

73. Additional reservations might refer to the need to set up a truly international and impartial body not beholden to any country or group of countries, nor acting on their behalf or behest, nor under their control but acting on truly humanitarian grounds. If such a body was ever set up (the UN given its decision-making structure where the SC rather than the General Assembly is more important, certainly does not qualify for being or ever becoming such a body) then forcible humanitarian intervention would gain wider and greater acceptance among states and peoples. But the principle of respecting the freedom of agency of a people still remains crucial.
74. See Vasant Kaiwar, 'The Aryan Model of History and the Oriental Renaissance' in Vasant Kaiwar and Sucheta Mazumdar (eds.), *Antinomies of History: Essays on Race, Orient, Nation*, Durham/London, 2003, p. 46.
75. In July 2019 the Modi government passed an Act deliberately and uniquely criminalising the Muslim male if he resorts to talaq or instant divorce though this had already been made illegal and liable to civilian penalties. On August 5, 2019 Article 370 was unconstitutionally annulled thereby eliminating the autonomy of J&K.

2

India's Constitution: How Democratic, How Just?

Wherein lies India's distinctiveness? Clearly no other country matches the scale of its religious, linguistic and ethnic diversity. Its racial heterogeneity is exceeded by a few West European and New World countries–the result of the colonial era experiences of conquest, the slave trade and resettlements as well as post-colonial migrations from the South to the North. While a major part of the scaffolding of caste–namely, such materially founded factors as kinship networks, status hierarchy, endogamy have existed everywhere and even notions of purity-impurity have been widespread–nowhere else but in this part of the world does there exist a system of such extreme gradations of human worth thanks to the ideological rationalization-stabilisation provided by Vedic inspired Brahminism.

India was not the only former colonial country that opted for a liberal-democratic political set-up following independence. Even so, the enormity of its territorial expanse, huge population, social diversity and economic backwardness, made it unique among democratic states. In the West, universal suffrage was extended to women and all races long after large-scale industrial and economic advancement had taken place. India, under vastly different circumstances erected a political framework based on democratic principles–and barring the 21-month Emergency, this framework, though battered has proved more resilient than early doomsayers had thought. It is part of the reason why the Constitution since its promulgation in 1950, commands such widespread admiration.

But now, almost seventy years later, and especially after the victory in the May 2019 general elections of the BJP and Sangh Parivar–a force that in word and deed has repeatedly demonstrated its antipathy to the progressive elements in the Constitution–it is time that a far more sceptical and critical eye be cast upon the foundational charter of the Republic.

Any evaluation of the Constitution cannot but be influenced by the political beliefs of the evaluator. Unlike liberals or social democrats, I believe that a more just, free, humane, egalitarian, democratic and ecologically sustainable country and world can only come about through the transcendence of capitalism and its associated political forms. I would contend that even a liberal democracy, in the pursuit of such a country and world, soon runs up against insurmountable limits. The belief that today's neoliberal capitalist order and the restricted freedoms and social benefits it allows can be substantially extended, or that its great inequalities of income, wealth and power can be dramatically reduced, is wishful thinking. The guiding vision for judging the Constitution should be one of a highly democratic and anti-bureaucratic socialism. But even those who do not share my vantage point, may be persuaded to find that even by the best standards said to be contained in the document–social justice and welfarism, liberal democratic freedoms, secularism–the Constitution is wanting.

How well the Constitution measures up to its stated aspirations, depends in large part on an evaluation of what it does to protect cultural and minority rights. This is a familiar standard for those of a liberal democratic worldview. But there is another criterion by which the Indian Constitution must also be judged: its commitment to the promotion and pursuit of social justice in a much wider sense, beyond just affirmative action for select groups. We need, then, to look at three things–the democratic content of the Constitution, its social-justice thrust, and the particular ways in which it addresses India's distinctiveness.

Recognising Deficiencies

Many claim that the Constitution is basically very good, but that its implementation has been flawed because of the ineptitude of politicians, bureaucrats and judges. Ambedkar is quoted as saying "however good a constitution may be, it is sure to turn out bad because those who are called to work it, happen to be a bad lot. However bad a constitution may be, it may turn out to be good if those called to work it, happen to be a good lot."[1] A more critical version upholding the same basic attitude will point to weaknesses, mainly of omission, whereby constitutional provisions understandably could not foresee or allow for future complexities and developments. But here too it is claimed that proper interpretation of the Constitution and implementation thereafter of its injunctions would constitute a major bulwark against democratic degeneration.[2]

This view flies in the face of how the Indian polity looks today. One cannot take refuge behind the argument that the Constitution—meant explicitly to shape all spheres of society—is blameless for the chasm between its good intentions and eventual societal outcomes. Around thirty per cent of the population is in absolute poverty. If we account for the costs of basic needs such as education, health care, social security and housing, another forty per cent or so fall under the category of what the late economist and former chairman of the National Commission for Enterprises in the Unorganised Sector, Arjun Sengupta called the "vulnerable poor," for whom the shock of a bad harvest, high inflation or an illness in the family can wreak havoc. Inequalities of income and wealth, and therefore of political power, are soaring. Hindu chauvinism, championed by the Sangh, has grown to be the single most dominant political ideal across the Republic, and the Bharatiya Janata Party, the Sangh's electoral arm, has achieved a truly national presence. Communal violence, previously episodic and larger in scale, since the Modi government came to power in 2014, has become smaller in scale but normalised and banal, with the police and courts doing little or nothing to stop or punish it. The one bright spot in India's trajectory over the last three decades is the political assertion of the oppressed castes, but even that is under constant assault and its future direction uncertain.

The Constitution is widely said to be a "living document"–one that not only shapes the evolution of Indian society, but is itself influenced by evolving societal trends and patterns. Hence it will not only express the parallelogram of forces created by the very mixed and conflicting intentions, beliefs and aspirations of the members of the original Constituent Assembly (CA) but will to some extent, greater or smaller, be shaped by the value outcomes emerging thereafter from subsequent contending socio-political forces. If some countries replace old constitutions with new ones to keep them relevant, in India keeping the Constitution "alive", has required a steady accumulation of amendments. (The country has had 103 constitutional amendments in 69 years, where Australia has had eight in a hundred years, and the United States 27 in over two hundred.) But have these changes, meant to address earlier flaws, shifted the Constitution in a more progressive direction, and by this helped to move ground reality in the same way? Given the overall and continuing authoritarian drift of the Indian polity and society–at the meso- and micro- levels it has always suffered from undemocratic, anti-social and brutal everyday practices–the answer is No!

A chronological study of the complex interplay between the respective trajectories of the Constitution and Indian society is a worthy enterprise. I do not propose to take that ambitious course here, but this two-way interaction underlies all the questions I ask of the document. How much concern, past or present, is there in the Constitution for issues of social justice, or for generating stronger movement in that direction? What kind of democracy has the Constitution sought to promote? How much responsibility, if any, does it bear for sanctioning the undeniable authoritarian drift of the polity over time?

The asymmetries of class power are obscured in the Constitution by propping up a notion of the "people's will," as expressed through electoral democracy. The Constitution is testament to the fact that the members of the original Constituent Assembly, incidentally not elected by universal suffrage, were overwhelmingly members of the Congress party–an organisation that headed an independence movement that sought not so much to overthrow colonial power, but to *transfer* it from British to Indian hands. It retains to this day, copious and detailed provisions for protecting the machinery of administration and governance. These were adopted almost intact from the Government of India Act of 1935–the colonial legislative instrument that preceded the Constitution. The senior advocate Rajeev Dhavan gives a somewhat cynical but not inaccurate portrayal of how the Constitution acquired its shape. "We the People of India," Dhavan writes, "who had little say in the making" of the document, "have been informed to accept this Constitution ... part of which is a British India clone," and which "makes unreal promises." Indians "have no choice but to accept this arrangement ... which our leaders have given to themselves to rule over us."[3]

From the beginning, the Constitution has carried Hindu, dominant-caste and patriarchal biases. (Not by coincidence– the members of the Constituent Assembly were overwhelmingly Hindu, upper-caste men.) For instance, in Article 1, the name given to the Union is "India, that is Bharat," invoking a pre-Islamic past of presumed glory–a *Bharat Varsha* when a legendary Hindu king is said to have ruled. Many of the Constitution's admirers–including such figures as the jurists Fali Nariman, H.M. Seervai, and Justice V.R. Krishna Iyer–do not appear to have drawn serious, let alone repeated, attention to these biases. Very few have dared to argue that the text exhibits any bias at all, thereby weakening its claim to secularity. One of those few is the scholar Pritam Singh, and this writer is indebted to his writings, particularly his paper "Hindu Bias in India's 'Secular' Constitution: probing flaws in the instruments of governance."[4]

These concerns are heightened today, as Indian progressives fear attempts by right wing groups to expand its control over state apparatuses and civil society. The Sangh, as Hindutva's fountainhead, is pushing a truly transformative project–the creation of a Hindu state in all but name–and has been unabashed about its desire to muster a two-thirds majority in both houses of parliament so as to amend the Constitution in line with its ambitions.

A number of liberal and even left voices have, in resistance, raised the slogan: "Defend the Constitution". This, as it stands, is inadequate. A more qualified and nuanced perspective and slogan is required: "Defend and deepen the progressive values and principles of the Constitution". This recognises the deficiencies in parts of the Constitution, but should still be a fitting rallying cry even for those liberals and social democrats whose admiration of the document is much less qualified than mine. And, should the Sangh ever succeed in amending the Constitution to further its anti-democratic aspirations, this slogan will retain its validity in the long term.

The underestimation of the communal and undemocratic features of Indian society has its parallel in the overestimation of the virtues of the Constitution. Given where India has come to stand, and as we look ahead, we must be clear-eyed about both.

Social Justice and Democracy

Given that there are different and contesting conceptions of justice, democracy and even disagreements about the value and scope of notions like 'social justice' one needs to mark out one's own perspective and relate that in critical or approving ways to the conceptions of these that are embodied in the Indian Constitution.

In contrast to the past when different religions provided the moral framework and injunctions for the regulation of everyday life generally subordinating women and rationalising existing social inequalities, it is with modernity that a more universal sense of both 'the common good' and of 'justice' emerges. This was due to the impact of the Enlightenment whose two main ideological legacies have been Liberalism and Socialism, the most egalitarian version of which has been Marxism. But, according to the philosopher Brian Barry, before the Industrial Revolution notions of justice pertained to individuals, and not to society.[5] It was about giving each their 'due' meaning not being cheated; getting a 'fair' price in a contract of buying/selling; of getting their desert, i.e., of merit; of appropriateness in that the punishment fits the crime–a corrective but not a seriously distributive conception of justice.

It has been superseded by the newer notion that inequality among humans is wrong–that all people equally are of worth. This is not the same as saying all people are of equal worth, but recognising a dignity in all individuals simply by virtue of their being humans. It follows that society must somehow be built on this new ideal which constitutes a very significant moral advance, and which requires reforming the 'basic institutions' that shape the provision and distribution of rights, opportunities and resources–be they the factory, market or state, going right down to families, schools, political parties and other civil associations. The question that remains is how inequalities of power, wealth and opportunity should be tackled. The answer has divided Liberals and Socialists.

An undisputed starting point is the need to ensure that all people have an equal opportunity to prosper. This does not, however, mean that a uniformity of outcomes is necessarily desirable. That is to say, there should be equal opportunities to become unequal. But then should *greatly* unequal outcomes be allowed to emerge? What limits, if any, should there be on inequality?

For right wing libertarians like Robert Nozick, redistribution through public takeover of private property is unjust because such private acquisition is a natural and therefore a moral right going beyond the issue of legality, although in capitalist societies such ownership of assets is legalized. Redistribution in the name of meeting social needs therefore cannot trump this basic freedom of ownership and is unjust, no matter the levels of inequality of wealth (and thus power) that exist. Socio-economic inequalities at birth, they would argue, are of no moral consequence since assets once acquired there is an automatic right and freedom of transfer and bequest. Only if original or subsequent accumulation of such family wealth was through unfair and duplicitous means can there be an attempt at redistributive rectification through precise identification and location of wrongdoing across generations; which is a complicated and tricky thing to do. If redistributive measures to rectify past injustices of this kind were attempted, the socio-political and negative costs of disrupting the present order of capitalism and its freedoms would be far too high. Best then, to let things be! Of course, contemporary accumulation through duplicitous means is another matter and would not be justified.[6]

The much-admired American liberal theorist John Rawls provides no real guide either on what should be done. His famous 'Difference Principle' holds that only those inequalities should be allowed that benefit the "least advantaged". As has been pointed out by Perry Anderson, this injunction is socially and politically indeterminate and quite capable of being interpreted to prioritise a regime of high and sustained inequalities as an incentive structure that promotes growth and thereby a greater 'trickle-down' to the most deprived.[7] For Rawls the subject of social justice is the basic institutions or in his words the 'basic structure of society' which allocate rights, opportunities and resources. For Barry, socialists must emphasize much more strongly not procedures to facilitate this but the justness of outcomes themselves. The focus should be not on institutions but on the rights, opportunities and resources themselves and their pattern of distribution to dramatically reduce inequalities.[8]

In identifying the spectrum of rights desirable there will not be complete agreement. Rights can and do clash because values clash! For liberals and even for social democrats, the 'right to property' even in the basic means of production will be seen as crucial for the pursuit of the common good. For the Marxist vision of socialism as common good, this is not the case. Many rights are institutionalised, i.e. having a right means one is 'free' or legally allowed (or not prevented) to do or have something. But there are rights that may not be legal, for example, customary or human rights whose proponents will push for being accepted and institutionalised. Having a right is one thing. Being able to exercise it by having the opportunity to do so is another. And in many cases even this is not enough. To fulfil the right and successfully use the opportunity will require resources. Where liberals, in talking of justice engage in a rights discourse, socialists, because they give greater importance to opportunities and resources will move for much more substantial change of the socio-political status quo.

Unlike liberals, socialists see a strong connection between the individual and larger groupings. This is not the same as in the case of multicultural enthusiasts where the preoccupation is the link between the individual and groupings, each defined by and differentiated from others, by specific cultural attributes. In contrast, the communities of belonging or association prioritised by serious socialists are perceived in social more than cultural terms and are numerically much broader, e.g. class. A *just* society is one which enables human flourishing because individual flourishing is inseparable from having a society of common good where all can flourish, and where the meaning to be given to the notion of flourishing is not 'happiness' but that each is better able to fulfil their distinctive potentials!

Must justice, to some extent, be trans-historical? Must we take responsibility for social injustices before our time? To a large extent, the answer is yes. We are born into unequal positions of power, wealth and status. For most people, what determines their social position in life is–in order of importance–inheritance, luck of birth, and merit (understood as the distance between one's starting and end point). Some groups such as lower castes have been so historically oppressed as to deserve *special* social, economic, political and educational support. Minority rights are not enough–opportunities and resources must come into the reckoning.

As with the issue of social justice let us now turn to the issue of democracy as a possible political-philosophical guide and criterion for assessing the Indian Constitution; a task made harder by the fact that the meaning of democracy is itself a contested terrain where one must choose one's particular vantage point.

In the conventional and dominant discourse on 'liberal democracy' the liberalism is given more importance than the democracy.[9] On one hand there is the classical understanding of democracy as 'rule by the demos' or popular empowerment in an ever-widening and deepening sense, i.e. democracy as always an 'unfinished business' wherein empowerment must go beyond the principles of political representation and accountability as well as civil liberties to encompass the social, economic and cultural domains of human existence. Political representation of the 'people' or citizenry is unavoidable in any democratic set-up but should be seen of as much a problem as it is deemed a solution.

Liberalism is about the restriction of state power for the presumed benefit of the individual where human fulfilment is essentially understood as the freedom to live as one desires as long as it does not impinge unfairly on others to do likewise. The key then is the construction of a legal-political framework that can provide 'equal basic liberties'. While this does not counter-pose or exclude, it does prioritise the more proceduralist domain of legal-political rights over the more substantive domain of the social and economic.[10] Democracy is or should be about the 'disalienation' of state power or the progressively greater capacity or power of people to take or influence the decisions that most affect one's lives within a collective framework of the pursuit of the common good. Here human fulfilment or flourishing is not seen as a privatised affair or pursuit.

If politics is best understood as *that dimension of social life that is concerned with arriving at, and giving effect to, collectively binding decisions and rules,* then the aim would be to achieve a much greater levelling of power equations; and far more decentralised, participatory and direct forms of decision-making alongside indirect structures and mechanisms of representative authority. Overall there would necessarily be a much stronger egalitarian dynamic that connects the nature of the political system with the system of economic production and distribution of resources. That is to say, such a democracy would seek to transcend the limitations of capitalism's separation of the economic and the political which has permitted important forms of political equality to emerge even as very significant levels of socio-economic inequalities of power and status remain or even deepen.[11]

While the dominant proceduralist conception held by liberals of what democratic freedom entails is valuable, because those legal commitments and procedures do themselves have a substantive content of importance, it can nevertheless be contrasted with a more substantive conception of democratic freedom that socialists of all hues ranging from Social Democrats to Marxists to Anarchists, would hold. For liberals, the key attributes that would define the democratic order are the following: (1) There must be free and fair elections with universal adult suffrage. (2) No arbitrary arrest but in accordance with the law and with the general presumption of innocence upheld by an independent judiciary. (3) There must be basic civil liberties, that is, the freedoms of speech/ assembly/association/religion/travel/residence/occupation/trade. These freedoms are not absolute but are subject to 'reasonable restrictions' as determined by the judiciary. (4) Existence of minority rights of varying scope.

In addition there should be a system of checks and balances through division of powers and responsibilities between the three main arms of the state–the executive, legislature and judiciary. Insofar as the democratic state operates within a single bounded territorial space (or even among two or more such non-contiguous but separately bounded spaces) there is unsurprisingly a relationship between its citizenry and nationalism whether the latter is understood as ideology, movement, sentiment or identity. Finally, there is an inescapable relationship of democracy with political secularism in that a state must not itself be subordinated to any religious body or its personnel, and that there must be equal citizenship rights for all, irrespective of religious affiliation. These equal citizenship rights may not be democratic however, e.g. Kemalist Turkey, Mao's China and Stalin's USSR. Thus, state secularity is the necessary but not sufficient condition for there being, in a minimalist and formal sense, a democratic state.[12]

Assessing the Constitution

From its beginning, the document betrayed its elitist character by placing some principles concerning socio-economic justice in the non-justiciable section of the Directive Principles, not in the binding Fundamental Rights. The Constitution's claim to a progressive social vision resides in these principles, yet the Directive Principles as a whole are best described as a basket of mostly worthy sentiments whose stimulus to goal fulfilment over the decades–the establishment of a meaningful welfare state, albeit capitalist–through the introduction of new laws, policies and their proper implementation, has been very weak.[13] This historical failure has diminished the stature of the Constitution, in concrete terms behaving more as a rationaliser of the status quo than as an instrument of progressive change.[14]

Bourgeois liberal democratic constitutions–and the Indian Constitution is certainly one–are always tolerant of serious class inequalities, usually defended as part and parcel of "basic liberties" that entail the right to private property and to accumulation in productive assets. In India, in the immediate aftermath of independence, given the widespread concern for social justice and therefore for land reform, an uneasy compromise took place. The right to "acquire, hold and dispose of property" was put into the fundamental rights but made subject to reasonable restrictions in the public interest. What pro-poor land reform measures took place was unevenly spread, limited and half-hearted. An Amendment in 1978 removed this right from Article 19 and made it a legal right only. Overall, there has been no real hindrance subsequently to the steady accumulation of private wealth. The expansion of the public sector and even the nationalisation of banks in earlier years have proven to be much more an aid to the growth of the capitalist class than a hindrance. Indeed, over the last three decades, the trend has been to de-nationalise and de-regulate productive assets. With respect to reducing class inequality, India has performed no better than other liberal democracies with explicit constitutional protections of private-property rights.

What does the Constitution have to say on caste inequality? Article 15 declares prohibition of discrimination on grounds that include caste. But this is with respect to state services and the domains of public control and administration. It does not extend to the sphere of ordinary and everyday social relations in Indian society as a whole. The Protection of Civil Rights Act focuses on untouchability. The Scheduled Castes and Scheduled Tribes (Prevention of Atrocities) Act has been in existence for over two decades, and was set up to check crimes against oppressed castes. These Acts are worthy measures but banning untouchability and merely condemning caste discrimination does not go far enough. There should, at the very least, be an unequivocal and comprehensive ban on caste discrimination, and the document should take a stand on eradicating the caste system itself, an imperative that should be included in the Directive Principles.

The fact that there has been no move to do this is revealing. It speaks of the nature of Indian secularism as it prevails in the Indian Constitution and is practised on the ground. Originally sanctioned by the predominantly dominant-caste Constituent Assembly, the current framework suggests that untouchability and even discrimination may disappear, but the caste system will remain intact. We must begin the debate on what steps should be taken to legislate against the caste system within the bounds of a democratic framework.

The Constitution itself affirms positive discrimination, in the form of caste-based affirmative action–through reservations for Scheduled Castes, Scheduled Tribes and Other Backward Classes. With the entrenched character of the caste system, this will remain a necessary means to counteract the caste system for many generations to come. Given this framework, it might be argued that a total ban on caste discrimination may not make total sense. But that does not hold water. A simple comparison with liberal constitutions in other countries indicates that it is possible to outlaw racial and gender discrimination even while governments pursue affirmative action along racial or gender lines as a means to ultimately ending such discrimination. India could very well do the same on caste.

On the issue of gender discrimination, the makers of the Constitution should have established a progressive Uniform Civil Code rather than the current mishmash of personal laws specific to–and conceding to–the traditional customs of each major religion. This would have been difficult given that the Congress's political mobilisation during colonial times rested on inter-religious collation, mediated in the Muslim case via Islamic clerics. But the party's immense prestige and authority as the undisputed leader of the freedom movement could have allowed it to impose uniform personal laws during negotiations in the Constitutional Assembly if its leadership really desired them. Of course, the non-secular and pro-Hindu character of much of this leadership at independence also had its part in determining the party's course. The Directive Principles include a call for a UCC, but this is another worthy sentiment which has never been seriously pursued. A few years later, Hindu Personal Law was substantially reformed to give women greater freedom and equality, but it is still a long way from granting women their rights in full. A gender-just UCC would require the abandonment of many current Hindu laws and practices regarding marriage, divorce, succession and matrimonial property, but India's political leaders, certainly not the BJP/ or Sangh, have never had much appetite to challenge all the prejudices of the country's dominant religious community. It would also mean attacking the status of the Hindu Undivided Family (HUF) which affords such families special tax breaks.

Instead, at the end of July 2019, the BJP succeeded in getting its triple talaq legislation passed in both houses of Parliament. It thus became an Act which is malevolently unique in being the first such law in India (or perhaps anywhere) which selectively *criminalises* the Muslim male for attempting to void marriage, a civil contract. According to certain forms of Islamic jurisprudence, the male partner could secure instant divorce through pronouncement in oral, written or electronic form of the Arabic word *talaq*, three times in quick succession. This practice was already struck down as illegal by the Supreme Court (SC). But now being made a criminal act, the Muslim man can be imprisoned for up to three years. This not only constitutes a vindictive and deliberate targeting of Muslim men, it also serves to divert attention away from the continuing need to establish an impartial gender just Civil Code covering women of all and no faiths.[15]

Regarding the upholding of adequate standards of liberal democratic functioning how strong are the Constitution's credentials?

How effective has the system of checks and balances between the legislature, the executive and the judiciary been?

The Indian Parliament does not enjoy the supremacy that Parliament has in the UK nor is it as independent from the executive as in the US. But it also does not exercise sufficient democratic control over the executive. This is due to powers constitutionally afforded to the latter–particularly the provisions for the executive to proclaim a state of emergency over the whole or part of the country, and thereby suspend fundamental rights. The imbalance is further abetted by a host of laws in the Indian Penal Code and elsewhere, that were inspired by colonial forms of rule. Measures for preventive detention, like the Unlawful Activities Prevention Act (UAPA), are used to restrict dissent, target political opponents and undermine progressive movements. In July 2019 the BJP government touched a new low through a successful amendment to the UAPA which allows an individual to be deemed a 'terrorist' if the National Investigation Agency (NIA) considers that person to be involved in 'preparing' or 'promoting' terrorism, while these two terms themselves remain utterly vague and imprecise in their meaning. This affords government agencies great interpretative ease in going after whomsoever they see fit such as those who–in another act of verbal creativity–are declared to be 'Urban Naxals'. Let us also not forget the colonial legacy which is still carefully nurtured, namely the laws against sedition. Furthermore, the central government, with the assent of the governor of a state–appointed by the central government–can declare President's Rule and dismiss the state's elected government. Laws such as these should simply be abolished.

Rather than function as a check on each other, the executive and parliament have all too often acted in cahoots. The task of making both organs accountable has fallen to the courts. The lower judiciary–magistrates and sessions' courts–is mostly suborned by local or provincial powers. Even at higher levels–High Courts and the Supreme Court–justice is all too often greatly delayed, and therefore denied. The higher courts can hold the executive accountable by supervising its work as well as setting up investigations into its behaviour. Despite this, the higher judiciary has been very lax when it comes to curtailing repressive laws and state actions.

There has been an ongoing tussle between the legislature and the judiciary as to which is the final arbiter of the Constitution. The Supreme Court's interpretation of the document has not been based solely on the text itself. Sometimes, it has aimed to give effect to the "intent" of the document's framers. Other times, the court has leaned towards "creative adaptation" of the document in the light of what it understands to be "Constitutional morality." The doctrine of the "basic structure" of the Constitution, formulated by the Supreme Court in 1973, has given the Court decisive and often controversial powers. The elected legislature, presumably representing the people, has the power to amend the Constitution, but the unelected Supreme Court, under the doctrine, has the power to annul any amendments that it deems to be violating the document's basic structure.

The Court has used its powers of interpretation to uphold progressive causes–as with the Right to Information Act, or its judgment on privacy being a part of Fundamental Rights. But should benches of the apex court act as guardians of the Constitution with only the Court's own higher benches able to check them? And what is to discipline and direct their power if there has never been judicial consensus on what all the basic features of the Constitution are, beyond certain generalities such as secularism, democracy, federalism, human rights, republicanism, rule of law, and so on? It is also alarming that there is neither sufficient transparency in appointments to the highest levels of the judiciary, nor any public accountability in how they reach their decisions.

Supreme Court judges, including chief justices, have played a part in legitimising the political behaviour and ideology of the Hindu right. The Court never demanded the removal of the Ram idols illegally installed in the Babri Masjid in 1949, and refused to authorise the use of security personnel under the central government to prevent the demolition of the mosque when petitioned to do so. In 1995, it ruled that Hindutva, far from being an anti-democratic ideology, was a "way of life." The most that can be said of the judiciary on this count is that it has sometimes acted to slow Hindutva's forward momentum–for matters would have been even worse in the absence of the basic structure doctrine and the Supreme Court's use of it to defend the Constitution.

Next, we must consider whether the parliamentary and party system defined by the Constitution fairly represent the popular will. Here too, there are weaknesses. Members of the Rajya Sabha do not need to be domiciled in the state they are supposed to represent. In parliament and state assemblies, members are not free to vote or abstain against their own party on any matter that the leadership claims is central to the party programme. Even to criticise one's party is extremely risky. The Anti-Defection law grafted on to the Constitution in 1985 has not succeeded in stemming frequent or mass defections for pecuniary and other reasons but it has seriously curtailed freedom of speech in Parliament. Legislators are fully protected from the courts and constitutional authorities by what they say and how they vote but not from their own party leaders. It makes obvious sense to prohibit voting against one's own party in the case of a motion of no confidence, but beyond that such enforced party obedience belittles rationality and quality in legislative argument and debate. What need for them if legislators cannot be persuaded to change sides or positions through the power of rational and persuasive argument?

What also of the recourse to referendums as a more direct form of popular empowerment and decision-making? Many countries have constitutions that allow for referendums within a carefully circumscribed range of issues, e.g. for constitutional amendments. In some cases these can take place at the provincial as well as at the central level. These referendums can be both non-binding and binding while in some countries they can be demanded by the public after a critical number of signatories are secured. The point is that allowing for the use of referendums expresses a desire for bringing in elements of direct democracy alongside the dominant indirect forms. It is certainly not to the credit of the Indian Constitution or to its makers, upholders and admirers that the issue of referendums and its circumscribed use at central and/or provincial levels has been completely ignored.[16]

However, what shines the harshest light on the Constitution's claim to democratic representation is the first-past-the-post (FPTP) electoral system. The justification so often peddled for it is that, in contrast to a system of proportional representation whether partial, mixed or full-blown, the first-past-the-post arrangement ensures a certain kind of stability.[17] The argument for FPTP is that it encourages a competitive two- or three-party system that lends itself to sturdy governments, rather than one with multiple contenders creating unstable coalitions that all too often do not last a full term in office. But stability is not a virtue in itself, and should not be allowed to trump proper representation of, and fidelity to, electoral choices. Moreover, coalitions have lasted their full terms both when ruling in individual states or at the Centre—in the case of the latter, on three consecutive occasions between 1999 and 2014.

Some kind of proportional representation would today provide an institutional bulwark against the undemocratic thrust of Hindutva. From independence up to the 2014 general election, whenever the country came under single-party majority rule, the winning side never had a majority vote share. Always, its share of the popular vote remained within the band of 40 to 49 per cent. In 2014, the concentrated support in the Hindi-speaking states for the Bharatiya Janata Party saw it secure a majority in the Lok Sabha with only 31 per cent of the vote and in 2019 with 37 per cent. This makes a mockery of any claim that these governments represented the popular mandate. It is also an insult to the Indian electorate. In 2014, excluding those who voted for independent candidates or for NOTA (None Of The Above), the votes of another 9 per cent of the public counted for nothing when in a PR system this would have resulted in a representative 48 seats in the Lok Sabha.

The Indian public's sheer political and social diversity is better reflected by the country's cornucopia of smaller regional parties, along with ones such as the Nishad Party, the Shiromani Akali Dal and the Maharashtrawadi Gomantak Party that have their bases in very particular social groups. These and the bigger but still regional parties might be expected, in their own interest, to call for proportional representation in the Lok Sabha, but the problem is that a similar system would then also have to be put in place for the state assemblies. This the stronger regional parties would not want, because it would dent their own hopes of securing state-level power—which rest, more often than not, on acquiring a disproportionately high number of seats in state assemblies vis-à-vis their actual vote share.

The Constitution's deficiencies when it comes to social justice and democratic governance have enabled Hindutva's ascension within the Republic. But the document also has two other grave flaws that have been wind in the sails of Hindu nationalism.

Two Grave Flaws

One flaw is shared with almost all constitutions everywhere. It is based on a self-serving understanding of the nation and nationalism. The nation with its associated sentiment of nationalist belonging is best understood as a *state of mind striving to become a political fact*. Thus it can emerge from nowhere as well as die out. Being a distinct nation involves seeking some degree of political control over a territorial space which can be a struggle for greater autonomy within a federation, to be part of a confederation, to merge with another existing state, or for becoming a separate nation-state with sovereign control over a bounded territory, i.e. secession. Virtually all constitutions, certainly the Indian one, will in the name of national consolidation and security, hypocritically allow for territorial *expansion* from original boundaries prevailing at their birth but will disallow any secession of territory.[18] India's Constitution took effect from January 1950. From that year onwards India acquired, in one way or the other, the Andaman and Nicobar Islands, Dadra and Nagar Haveli, Goa, Pondicherry and Sikkim.

Constitutions are one-sided in this respect (allowing territorial boundaries to expand but not retreat) partly because they assume that all secessionism stems from some external attack or influence. They are generally blind to the notion that territorial unity is not an incontestable virtue in itself, but that its virtue is always subordinate to the voluntary and continuous assent to membership of a territorial unit from all of its constituent parts. That assent is never to be taken for granted. When substantial sections of people in a given province or region do not wish to be part of the Union–because of a pre-colonial history of separateness from the constituents of the new country, or because they suffer from disregard or even repression by the country's rulers–then the call can arise for respecting their "right to self-determination, even and up to secession" (Lenin's classic democratic formula). There are only a few governments that are prepared to consider or accept such a call by a section of their citizenry, even as their constitutions do not inscribe this highly democratic principle. Former Czechoslovakia quietly became the Czech Republic and Slovakia; East Germany merged with West Germany; referendums were held in Quebec and Scotland to ascertain public sentiments for staying within Canada and the United Kingdom respectively, and it is quite possible for Scotland to peacefully break away via another referendum in the future.

India practises an asymmetrical federalism, one where all the states in a Union do not have the same legislative powers. Put another way, some states have special ad hoc powers denied to the others. This kind of federalism often emerges from the dissolution of colonial empires whose masters did not administer their territorial units through uniform rules and procedures. In both Nagaland and Kashmir, the Indian government after independence has behaved atrociously in denying the aspirations of their respective populations. Long-standing repression has succeeded in ending the Naga quest for independence, now replaced by a search for some degree of autonomy. Kashmir is another story.

The exact circumstances under which the princely state of Jammu and Kashmir acceded to the Indian union, and whether the Indian state was involved in duplicity, are a matter of dispute.[19] Not under dispute are the legal and formal commitments India made for the accession to take place. Jammu and Kashmir would have its own flag and premier, and its own constituent assembly to draw up its own constitution. The original arrangement was much more a "confederal" than a federal one–only the territory's foreign affairs, defence and communications came under the control of the Centre. Jammu and Kashmir was not to be bound by any future Indian Constitution since it could have its own. But since Presidential orders can be used to bring in terms set by the Indian Constitution through "consultation" or "concurrence" with the state government, the key path for central efforts to undermine the original intent and spirit supposedly embodied in Article 370 lay in having obedient state governments in J&K.

What followed is a sorry tale of repression. In 1953, Sheikh Abdullah, the territory's popular leader, was arrested and replaced as premier by the Centre's toady, Bakshi Ghulam Mohammed. Manipulation of the Jammu and Kashmir constituent assembly diluted earlier commitments to maximum autonomy, and instead allowed the imposition of Union powers. Those articles of the Constitution were made applicable to Jammu and Kashmir that allowed the central government to dismiss an elected state government as well as assume its legislative functions. In the time of Jawaharlal Nehru and afterwards, Jammu and Kashmir's autonomy was systematically eroded as the region came under the jurisdictions of the Indian Administrative Service, the Indian Police Service, the Election Commission and the Supreme Court.

Jammu and Kashmir has suffered repeatedly from president's rule and governor's rule, easily exceeding 3,000 days and is currently still under such rule. The single longest continuous stretch of such rule (well over six years) has happened in Jammu and Kashmir between January 1990 and October 1996. Between 1947 and 1964, all except three of the 97 subjects in the Union list which allows the Parliament to make laws, 26 of the 47 in the Concurrent list which includes subjects that give power to both the state and central government, and 260 out of 395 articles from the Indian Constitution were extended to Jammu and Kashmir. Then and subsequently, repressive acts such as the Armed Forces (Special Powers) Act, Public Safety Act and Terrorist and Disruptive Activities (Prevention) Act were brought into play.

No arm of the democratic Indian polity–whether the legislature, executive, judiciary or any opposition party–has seen fit to seek a reversal of this systematic erosion, let alone a restoration of earlier commitments. The territorial 'unity and integrity' of the country is paramount regardless of what the public, particularly in the predominantly Muslim Kashmir Valley, may want. The land is more important than the people!

Finally, on August 5, 2019 the BJP and Sangh carried out what it had long promised to do, namely abrogating Article 370 itself. This was done through a brazen violation of the Constitution. The fundamental basis on which the region was incorporated into the Union was through the sovereign authority of a J&K Constituent Assembly set up in 1951 and permanently dissolved in 1957. While a state legislature–which can never have sovereign authority but only a representative authority–was repeatedly used to make modifications and shift more and more powers embodied in the Indian Constitution to the province, the annulment of Article 370 can only be done by that J&K Constituent Assembly. To get around this, the Modi government used another Article 367 to introduce a clause to make J&K's state legislature the equivalent of its constituent assembly. Then if a state assembly is not in operation because, for example, President's Rule has been imposed, (Central rule was imposed on J&K on June 20, 2018 and repeatedly extended since then) this allows the President to usurp the powers of this assembly and issue ordinances that become law. Given this unconstitutional equation of two fundamentally different assemblies, the next step was then to nullify Article 370 followed by a historically unprecedented act–downgrading the status of J&K from statehood to that of two separate Union Territories of J&K and Ladakh respectively. Thereafter, Article 35A which prevented private land sales or state government posts to those not domiciled in J&K was scrapped.

In the days before the August 5 announcement the Modi government sent an extra 38,000 troops to join the already over 750,000 armed personnel already stationed in the Valley. A communications lockdown (no landline or mobile phone service or internet availability for the general public) was put in place as also strict curfews, and the banning of any public assembly of more than 5 people while house arrests of local party leaders was also carried out. These measures have broadly remained in place for well over six months with no signs as yet of complete removal while hospital reports of gun pellet injuries and ruthless beatings of stray civilians by the army during this period are basically ignored in the media outside Kashmir.

The issue has already been taken to the Supreme Court. Should it not reverse this unconstitutional annulment (which is almost certain) then this too will speak volumes about how the supreme guardian of the Constitution is itself willing to betray its primary role! It may, although this too is unlikely, overturn the arbitrary downgrading to UT status of one or both the parts. If the SC does not strike this down it will have set a dangerous precedent whereby the President, at the behest of the PM and Cabinet, can dramatically accelerate much greater centralization of power in New Delhi vis-à-vis all other states within the Union. The implications for the nature of Indian federalism as laid down in the Constitution will then be profound. As it is, the SC on August 13 endorsed for a further period the arbitrary military clampdown on the Valley which violates the fundamental rights of the people there. Despite habeas corpus petitions challenging detentions by the government, the SC acted in a manner that exempted the government from its constitutional obligation to explain itself instead calling on the petitioners to go to Kashmir to meet the alleged detainees.[20]

The other area that warrants deeper analysis is the Constitution's claim to secularism and therefore to democracy. How far should the state intervene in religious practices that many would consider morally offensive? Some general principles can help guide us at least. There are certain basic individual rights of equality across caste, gender and racial lines that must take priority over group rights. There must also be the "right of exit" for individuals from religious groups or injunctions felt as demeaning or imposed. None of this is to be taken as meaning that the principle of minority rights is to be rejected. The principle remains fundamental to any democratic set-up. So the attack on "minorityism" by Sangh spokespersons is to be completely rejected even as we can of course oppose specific abuses by those enjoying such rights. Religious bodies must also be pushed to change older injunctions in the light of modern democratic and humane values.

But countries believing themselves to be secular, must also be careful in how they address the issues of religious freedoms and personal choices even when these are to some extent the result of socialisation processes. For example, India sensibly enough and unlike certain European democracies has not, in the name of upholding secular principles, gone to the absurd extent of outlawing certain forms of dress by Muslim women such as the hijab, burqa or niqab when worn in public. Apart from certain professions as in medicine or teaching where full face-to-face interaction with patients and students may be required, there is no justification for such bans. Rather, there should be a ban on the forcible imposition of such apparel by families or communities. The basic and innocuous freedom to dress as one wishes, should be respected.[21]

Many progressives have pointed out that there is a disturbing gap between the secular principles laid down in the Constitution and their practice on the ground. This serves as an exculpation of sorts for the Constitution, but an unconvincing one. The fact is that the text of the document is itself religiously biased. In the name of freedom of religion, the Constitution allows educational institutions set up by any particular religious denomination, sect or body to provide religious instruction to students, even if the institution is partially–though not fully–funded by the state. Moreover, it says that if an educational institution set up by an endowment or trust that insists on imparting religious instruction is taken over by the state, such instruction can continue at the institution. A forthright secular stand would be for the state to refuse both these things: to not provide any funding to such institutions; and to refrain from taking over institutions that insist on specific religious instructions. However, the most prodigious biases are those in favour of Brahminical Hinduism.

I have already mentioned the Constitution's effective sanction for the persistence of the caste system, with its untenable position that this is quite compatible with ending untouchability and caste discrimination. I have also mentioned its controversial choice of the name "Bharat." There is more to add to this set of faults.

In the Constitutional Assembly debates, B.R. Ambedkar defined religious freedom as entailing only the freedom to worship, and excluding all practices outside of that act. Such a definition would have created grounds to oppose Hindu practices such as sati and child marriage. The final definition of religious freedom in Article 25 of the Constitution reflected a compromise. It enshrined the freedom to practice and propagate religion, "Subject to public order, morality and health." Given the wide latitude in how this clause can be interpreted, it is no surprise that many an unsavoury religious practice persists without state intervention.

Brahminical diehards in the Constitutional Assembly could not get a complete ban on cow slaughter, but smuggled an emphasis on the need to protect cows into the Directive Principles under the cover of animal husbandry. The overwhelming majority of states have since banned cow slaughter, and a few have even banned the killing of bulls and bullocks.

Many states have banned conversions if done by force, fraud or allurement. These bans are aimed at Islam and Christianity, since there is much eye winking at Hindu conversions passed off dishonestly as "reconversions" to the ostensibly "original" faith. The ban on forcible conversion is justified, but the two other grounds for prohibition allow for unwarranted state interference on flimsy grounds. Many Hindutva stalwarts have said that Christian beliefs in heaven and hell constitute fraud. The prohibition on conversion via allurement is particularly directed at progressive missionary groups setting up civic institutions such as schools and hospitals in tribal and other underserved areas. This as a criterion for preventing conversions should simply be dismissed. Advertising allurement is central to the functioning of a capitalist economy. And there is little check on whether claims made for their efficacious effects are all true or fraudulent. People also believe and convert for material reasons and hopes. There are numerous sects in various religions (including many Hindu sects) worldwide which win loyalties because they provide for welfare needs, while others claim to provide forms of therapy mental and spiritual.

Article 25, while establishing the freedom of religion, also states in a sub-clause that this freedom shall not prevent the state from making any law for "the throwing open of Hindu religious institutions of a public character to all classes and sections of Hindus." The document notes that, in the sub-clause, "the reference to Hindus shall be construed as including a reference to persons professing the Sikh, Jain or Buddhist religion." Here, the Constitution can be seen as almost in line with Hindutva's assimilationist project, which sees these faiths as having a lineage that goes back to ancient India, and being given shape by Hinduism, which preceded it. Unlike Christianity, Zoroastrianism, Islam and Judaism these faiths are indigenous, not "foreign" and therefore acceptable, in the Hindutva view. Within the Sangh Parivar it is common to find references to Sikhs as protectors of Hindus against Mughal/Muslim oppression. Jains have been seen as a part of the wider Hindu fold. As Sikh and Jain identity has crystallized, this assimilationist attitude has caused some degree of resentment but this Hindutva position also ensures that Sikhs and Jains need have no or much less fear of a rising Hindutva. Ambedkar's counter positioning of Buddhism to Hinduism has made little ground even as Dalit assertion has strengthened.

Article 26 allows every religious denomination to "establish and maintain institutions for religious and charitable purposes, but clause 2(a) of Article 25, saves the power of the state to regulate or restrict "any economic, financial, political or other secular activities which may be associated with religious practice." It can oversee the construction of facilities and look into the spending of monies given by devotees, and even ratify the qualifications of priestly candidates. Article 26 is seemingly impartial towards all religious institutions, but in reality a huge and powerful nexus has emerged between the state, the corporate sector and the Hindu religious establishment. The writer Meera Nanda, in her book *The God Market: How Globalization is Making India More Hindu*, provides a devastating exposé of this nexus.[22]

Sikh affairs are governed by the 1925 Sikh Gurudwaras Act, Muslim mosques and charities are largely unified under the 1954 Wakf Act, and Protestant and Orthodox Christian churches obey the National Council of Churches, set up in 1914 while Catholic churches also have their overarching authorities. But the thousands of Hindu sects lack any single authority to watch over them. State governments have set up various regulatory bodies to oversee the affairs of Hindu, Jain and Buddhist temples.

The Constitution designates Hindi the "official language of the Union," to be used along with English in Centre-state exchanges. Though Hindi is spoken by more people than any other Indian language–even as we ignore that a Hindi nationalism has been at work, wherein other north Indian languages have been subsumed by Hindi and rendered as dialects–it is still spoken by a minority of the country's entire population.[23] Achieving this status had not a little to do with north Indian and upper caste dominance of the Constituent Assembly. The Constitution also grants official status to Sanskrit, spoken by a perhaps few hundred people, by including it in the Eighth Schedule. The tribal languages of Bhili and Lammi, each spoken by over a million people, are denied that honour. Article 351 promotes a Sanskritised Hindi that relies for its vocabulary "primarily on Sanskrit and secondarily on other languages." The promotion of Hindi comes at the expense of Hindustani, which affords greater importance to Urdu with its stronger Persian and Arabic borrowings.

The Indian state, at the central and state levels, promotes the propagation of Hindu priest craft through *gurukuls*, *rishikuls* and *pathshalas*, and "Vedic sciences" through astrology courses at the college level. Governments sell lands at throwaway prices, or outright gift them, to Hindu religious bodies for the construction of schools, hospitals and other institutions, to which the state also provides patronage and accreditation. These are then built and maintained by private and corporate donations. The end result has been a growing trespass of Hindu institutions into such supposedly secular areas as public education and health.

In Conclusion

At its very creation, the Indian Constitution was never the remarkable document many have claimed it to be. Its commitment to secularism, liberal freedoms and social justice was never wholehearted, and was more restricted than it needed to be. The end goal of its "transformative vision" was the establishment of a welfarist, capitalist democracy, and the society that has emerged over time under its aegis has neither formally repudiated this goal nor come close to achieving it. Instead, we have arrived at a neoliberal capitalism which is averse to serious welfare provisions for the general public; that allows large-scale poverty to persist; and inequalities of wealth and power to reach obscene levels.

Indian democracy, though it long enjoyed a relative stability in its macro-level structures and institutions, has forever tolerated violence and a lack of democratic practices at its middle and lower levels. Over the last three decades, things have turned for the worse. The legislature, executive, judiciary and the media have been gradually hollowed out through partisan appointments and corruption, including by the government itself. Worst of all, the country's single most dominant political force is now the Sangh Parivar, a far-right force with undeniable fascist characteristics. Other such forces are resurgent across the world, but, unlike them, in the RSS, the Sangh has a continuous existence of over 90 years. The Sangh's hegemonising drive will continue as it always has, with greater or lesser success, irrespective of the ups and downs of electoral verdicts. Its cadres and institutions have implanted themselves in Indian society at a depth unmatched by any rival, and key components of the Sangh's own transformative vision for the country have found resonance among a wide public—even among many opposition parties that otherwise oppose the idea of a Hindu Rashtra.

What are some of the key themes of this growing public 'common sense'? One, that there is no alternative to a neoliberal economic order, and that the only question for economic debate is whether this should take a more disciplinary or compensatory form depending on the prevailing balance of social forces. Another, more directly spawned by Sangh success, is that any party aspiring to electoral success must pander to the Hindu majority, distancing itself from even the suggestion that it appeases religious minorities and adopt to a greater or lesser extent various aspects of the Hindutva worldview. Furthermore, that there is no escape from playing on the same ground as the BJP and Sangh–we are all for a more belligerent and militaristic nationalism and for asserting our regional dominance as the path to achieving the status of a rising global power.

There are enough positive aspects of the Constitution for us to take selective recourse to it in the struggle against the Sangh. But, we must ask, how well does the document stand against the new common sense seeping into ever more sections of the public?

The centre of gravity of Indian politics has moved very much to the right. The Congress is not a far-right force, but long ago transmogrified into an ugly right wing force. It has no inspiring transformative vision of its own. Constructing a counter to the Sangh will require a search for new ways on all fronts–economic, political, social, cultural and ideological. Greater success in that struggle must precede the further evolution of a Constitution–to be 're-constituted', as it were–so that it can deliver more to the people of India than it yet has.

Notes

1. See Madhav Khosla, *The Indian Constitution*, OUP, New Delhi, 2012, p. 164. But even while recognising the value of this admonition, Khosla would not place so much emphasis on the power of individuals.
2. See Samir K. Das, "The Founding Moment: Social Justice in the Constitutional Mirror" in Ashok Agrwaal and Bharat Bhushan (eds.) *State of Justice in India*, Sage Publishers, New Delhi, 2009. Das claims that the Constitution has 'multifarious concepts of

justice' and cites Granville Austin's famous 1966 text *The Indian Constitution: Cornerstone of a Nation* in defence of this argument.

3. Rajeev Dhavan, *The Constitution of India: Miracle, Surrender, Hope*, Universal Law Publishing (Lexis Nexis), Sahibabad, 2017, pp. 36 and 37.
4. This first appeared in *Third World Journal*, Vol. 26, No. 6, 2005.
5. Brian Barry, *Why Social Justice Matters*, Polity Press, Cambridge UK, 2005.
6. Robert Nozick, *Anarchy, State and Utopia*, Basic Books, 1974. See G.A. Cohen, 'Nozick on Appropriation' in *New Left Review*, March-April, 1985 for a severe critique of Nozick on this. Also important is Cohen's 'Freedom, Capitalism and Justice' in *New Left Review*, March-April 1981.
7. Perry Anderson, *Spectrum*, Verso, 2005, Chapter 4.
8. What distinguishes Barry (and others like him) from Marxists is their continued faith in the reformability of basically capitalist social relations to achieve their desired goal of a strongly social democratic capitalism that is also ecologically sustainable. The socialism of Marxists sees this as a chimera, more so given the global transition of nation-states towards a meaner and more unequal than ever neoliberal capitalist order whereby ecological devastation has accelerated.
9. See Ellen Meiksins Wood, *Democracy Against Capitalism*, Cambridge University Press, 1996.
10. Hence in Rawl's 'two principles of justice' giving lexical priority to this over his 'difference principle' dealing with the domain of the socio-economic inequalities. Not only is it the case that the pursuit of 'basic sufficiencies' has marked much more the course of human history than the pursuit of 'basic liberties' but that the actual content or capacity to benefit from a regime of equal basic liberties is seriously diminished by the persistence of great socio-economic inequalities. It is an elementary truth that in capitalist societies, greater wealth translates into greater political power and influence. Amartya Sen has sought to capture this in his definition of 'development as freedom', i.e. of people having the material and ideational capabilities "to lead the lives they

have reason to value and to enhance the real choices they have." Amartya Sen, *Development As Freedom*, OUP, 1999, p. 293.

11. In capitalism unlike pre-capitalist agrarian societies, the separation of the economic and political means that political and economic elites are not congruent and do not strongly map on to each other. This allows for the possibility of liberal democracy wherein civic-political equality can co-exist with unequal economic power. The ruling class in capitalism is the first class that does not directly govern! Permitting is not the same as enabling. Everywhere liberal democratic rights and practices emerge because of struggles from below.
12. There are also political scientists who argue that a democratic state need not be secular, while others would see a strong and fundamental overlap between secularism and democracy. Adherents of the first view include Robert Dahl, *Polyarchy*, Yale University Press, 1971, Arendt Lijphart, *Patterns of Democracy*, Yale University Press, 1999, Alfred Stepan, "The Multiple Secularisms of Modern Democratic and Non-Democratic Regimes' in Craig Calhoun, Mark Juergensmeyer, Jonathan Van Antwerpen (eds.), *Rethinking Secularism*, OUP, 2011. This view allows for defence of Israel (an explicitly Jewish state with formally constituted second-class citizenship rights for non-Jews) to be called a democracy. For a powerful rebuttal of such a view of Israel see the public speech of the late Ronald Dworkin available at 'E.H. Thompson Forum on World Issues (2008)' on youtube.com. On the other side there is Rajeev Bhargava who says freedom to follow your religion and equality of citizenship rights regardless of religious affiliation (which can characterize an authoritarian but secular regime like the former Soviet Union or Kemalist Turkey) is not enough. For him a secular state "is committed to a more general freedom and equality." There must be "equality of *free* citizenship" [my emphasis]. Rajeev Bhargava, 'India's Secular Constitution' in Achin Vanaik and Rajeev Bhargava (eds.) *Understanding Contemporary India: Critical Perspectives*, Orient Blackswan, 2010.
13. While Nehru's vision of socialism was precisely this welfarist capitalism, the fact that the term socialism did not feature in the

preamble is indication enough that the consensual position in the CA was not a serious commitment to its pursuit. As for believing in Mrs. Gandhi's sincerity of commitment to this vision when she introduced the term into the preamble during the Emergency, the less said the better.

14. In 2009 the Right To Education (RTE) Act was passed and came into force the next year. The Centre and states were put under the obligation to provide "free and compulsory" elementary education for 6 to 14 year olds. The Constitution in Article 45 in the DP already had called for this fulfilment in ten years after the commencement of the Constitution. It is sixty years later that this commitment was shifted from the DP to being a fundamental right. But this certainly does not mean that the provision of such education has become universal, let alone that it is everywhere of minimally decent quality with properly trained teachers and adequate facilities in place. For those social rights not included in the FR, Indian laws and SC rulings only recognize a violation if the State has announced a scheme for some beneficiaries but does not fulfil them or denies it to identified beneficiaries. There is no obligation of the state to meet such social rights.
15. Obviously it is the gender-just character of the UCC and not the uniformity aspect of it that is crucial. The state of Goa has a common civil code that is secular and accepted by all religious communities there. It was imposed by Portuguese rule in 1910 and remains after its incorporation into the Union of India. It needs updating to take into consideration more modern forms of property ownership as well as more egalitarian principles guiding conjugal relationships and their possible break-ups. But it stands an example of a step that could have been taken when drafting the Constitution and of its durable acceptance by religious communities.
16. See 'Referendums by Country–Wikipedia'. Well over twenty democracies have constitutional provisions for the selective use of referendums, in some cases on demand by a critical public mass. Austria, Sweden and Switzerland have both binding and non-binding referendums depending on the issue or law. Switzerland

and Canada have it at central and provincial levels, in the former case also at the municipal level. Subject to a minimum number of petitioners Venezuela has recall referendums for elected officials up to and including the President.

17. Proportional representation by the single transferable vote would be ideal assuming a threshold of 2 per cent of total votes to be crossed for parliamentary presence. Voters list their candidate/ party preferences and should that first choice party overall not cross the threshold, then votes are transferred to the lower chosen preferences.
18. The Indian Constitution helps to "uphold the belief that almost all practices of power directed to maintaining the unity and integrity of the nation are inherently justice enhancing." Upendra Baxi, 'The Impossibility of Constitutional Justice' in Z. Hasan, E. Shridharan and R. Sudarshan, *India's Living Constitution: Ideas, Practices, Controversies*, Permanent Black, 2002, p. 37.
19. See Christopher Snedden, *Understanding Kashmir and Kashmiris*, Speaking Tiger Publications, 2017, Part III.
20. There is a scathing indictment of the SC accepting "executive supremacy by stealth" in Gautam Bhatia's article "The absentee constitutional court" in *The Hindu*, September 12, 2019.
21. But this is qualitatively different from affording a special privilege to a particular religious group to publicly carry, as a matter of religious right, a potentially lethal weapon such as a kirpan. In fact, many devout Sikhs either keep a symbolic inscription of the kirpan in say a comb or do not carry a kirpan at all.
22. Random House, India, 2009. See especially Chapter 3 on "The State-Temple-Corporate Complex and the Banality of Hindu Nationalism".
23. See Alok Rai, *Hindi Nationalism*, Orient Longman, 2002; and David Lelyveld, 'Words as deeds: Gandhi and language' in P. Brass and A. Vanaik (eds.), *Competing Nationalisms in South Asia*, Orient Longman, 2002.

3

India's Two Hegemonies

Despite long-standing Indian ambitions no government has been able to exercise hegemony let alone domination over all the countries that make up South Asia. Yes, Sikkim was swallowed up in 1975 and Bhutan behaves obediently although not happily whenever New Delhi demands as much. But Bangladesh, Sri Lanka and Nepal are neither allies nor enemies but always wary neighbours. The main although not only obstacle to such ambitions to achieve a stable pre-eminence befitting the status of a would-be regional hegemon has always been Pakistan. Even in respect of coercive power, the military balance between the two countries only moved in favour of India after Pakistan's dismemberment in 1971 leading to the independence of Bangladesh. But India's ability to take political-military advantage of this was first reduced by the subsequent Shimla Accord (1972) returning captured Pakistani soldiers en masse; and then effectively nullified in 1998 by India's initiation of mutual subcontinental nuclearization. Realistically speaking, political forces aiming to secure, sustain and expand hegemonic influence have had to operate at the domestic level. Not only in India but most everywhere these, in recent times, have taken form of rightwing authoritarian populisms.

Among the right wing strongmen enjoying broad electoral support today, Narendra Modi commands a position in India at least as sweeping as that of Erdoğan in Turkey, or Duterte in the

Philippines. Like them, he glories in being a plebeian upstart with a thuggish base, though he rules a country of nearly 1.3 billion people, a sixth of the world's population. Since his victories in 2014 repeated with an even stronger electoral mandate in the 2019 general elections, Modi's BJP has enjoyed unchallenged dominance of the national-political scene: an overall majority in both Houses of Parliament, buttressed by control of the largest provincial state legislatures. The BJP's nearest rival, the once all-powerful Congress Party, has been reduced to less than a tenth of Lok Sabha seats and governs only a handful of states. Indeed the scale of BJP hegemony today can bear comparison to that of the Indian National Congress party in the first decades after independence, under Jawaharlal Nehru and his daughter, Indira Gandhi. Then, too, a single party with a charismatic figurehead commanded the national scene and predominated at state-provincial level.

What sort of rupture do these new hegemons represent with the more reverential forms of bourgeois rule that went before? The best way to grasp the novelty of India's new regime may be to compare its mode of operation to that of Congress. Electorally, the pattern is clear: an era of single-party Congress rule from independence in 1947 to the late 1960s, followed by its steady decline and increasing resort to coalition governments; a long interregnum, with the upward trajectory of the BJP and its allies beginning in the late 1980s, after the brief fillip for Congress in 1984, following Indira's assassination; and the restoration of a single-party majority by the BJP under Modi in 2014, thirty years later. Between the two eras lies a major shift in the political-economic epoch, from the statist developmentalism of the post-war decades to a globalized neoliberalism since the 1990s, reflected in the programmes of both parties; and with it, a dramatic though uneven advance of different caste and class fractions. Here as elsewhere the main political trend, to borrow a phrase from Stuart Hall, has been 'the great moving right show'. The BJP is no ordinary party: its nervous system is supplied by a 1930s-style, uniformed, hard-line Hindu-nationalist cadre force, the RSS, which also controls a wide array of civil-society organizations, known collectively as the Sangh.[1] Yet this makes its rise as a second all-India hegemon all the more striking. How do the dynamics of the two compare, in terms of national ideologies, party forms, leading figures, class alliances, patterns of rule? This essay will look at the similarities and contrasts between them, and at the passage from the first to the second. For if, in a negative sense, the decline of Congress created the space for the rise of Hindutva forces, in key respects it also paved their way.

1. Hegemony of Congress

To secure a hegemonic bourgeois bloc requires stability at three levels: control over those below, through whatever shifting mix of sticks and carrots; successful arbitration between ruling-class fractions—which in India, still 70 per cent rural, also means effective handling of tensions created by the agrarian bourgeoisie; and a sufficient degree of support from the professional and petty-bourgeois middle classes. As Gramsci pointed out, there is no hegemony without the effort to forge a national-popular will. A successful hegemonic ideology will mask contradictory interests while offering some 'unified' sense of belonging to the majority. This is where nationalism comes in, calling for subordination to a 'higher' cause or promising benefits to 'true nationals', and thereby reconciling otherwise clashing interests. In the Indian context, fighting on the terrain of nationalism has involved securing mass support for one's particular vision of 'India's' cultural and political content. Both the RSS and the Congress emerged as mass-political projects in the inter-war period, and confronted the problem of forging a national-popular will for self-determination against British colonial rule.[2] Though their constructions of what Indian nationalism was supposed to mean had differing inflections, they came from a shared starting point.

The Idea of 'India'

Nineteenth-century stirrings of Indian national consciousness drew upon a Romantic-Orientalist nationalist historiography crafted by upper-caste Hindus, which glorified an 'ancient'—that is, pre-Muslim–'Hindu' India and denigrated the long centuries of Muslim rule before the arrival of the enlightened British. In the run-up to independence, both versions of Indian nationalism foregrounded the religious divide. But 'communal' nationalists saw the Mughal era as a foreign-imposed dark age, and the 'unity of Hindus' as the paramount principle on which a strong India must be built. A 'softer' variant, taken up by the Congress leaders, called for a religiously brokered Hindu-Muslim pact, based on 'unity in diversity'. Though Nehru saw virtues in the Mughal rule of Akbar, for most Hindu intellectuals the key factor was the supposedly unique tolerance, goodness and accommodating character of Hinduism, which would enable the development of a composite Indian culture, in turn founding a composite nationalism. Since this accommodating spirit was allegedly ancient, it had to pre-date the coming of Islam and thus once again afforded a special status to a Vedic-inspired Hinduism. This helped to create the myth that, despite the deep entrenchments of caste and wide variations in religious practice, Hinduism constituted a single if mosaic-like faith, the 'mosaic' itself being testimony to its inherent tolerance.[3] This was the basis of the 'secular' Indian nationalism propounded by the Congress leadership, who presented it as founded on a deep, impartial respect for all religious communities–as if imbalances in numerical and power terms would not count.[4] It was, effectively, 'majoritarian nationalism in a liberal garb'.[5] During the independence struggle, both versions therefore allowed Hinduism's symbols and myths to be deployed for the purposes of popular mobilization; the Gandhi-led Congress made no such use of Muslim symbols.[6]

If Congress predominated with ease over the fractured political landscape of 1930s India–winning nearly half the seats in the limited-franchise 1937 provincial elections, for example–this was in part because its leaders had established themselves as key interlocutors for the British authorities, and took care to damp down any mass mobilizations which threatened that position. By contrast, the Indian Communist Party was banned till 1942, and its militants were executed or imprisoned. The Sangh, for its part, largely stayed away from the independence struggle, preferring to cultivate its 'purity'; the RSS was briefly banned after an ex-member assassinated Gandhi in 1948, but legalized in 1949 by the Home Minister Sardar Patel, more hostile to the Communists than to the 'patriotic if misguided' RSS. As for Congress itself, leadership of the national movement had endowed the party with immense prestige and mass credibility in the first decade after independence, which also supplied its major ideological adhesive. This was the era in which the Nehruvian Consensus held sway—in reality, a mishmash of developmentalist goals, vague ideals and nationalist themes, such as modernization, 'scientific temper', industrialization, socialism (in the sense of welfarist capitalism), democracy and non-alignment, combined with Indian national unity and the Hindu-tilted 'secularism' described above. This secularism had little real resonance on the ground; belief in it served more to delude Congress under Nehru that its official nationalism had deep historical roots and thus a strong hegemonic dynamic as well. It did not.[7] Once independence was achieved, the Congress's ideological porosity became more apparent. If it exercised a sustained hegemony over the next decades, this was due less to its ideology than to more material factors: developmentalism, the first-past-the-post electoral system, the advantages of incumbency and neutralization of any communist threat.

Among these, the developmental promise of Nehruvianism had the greatest public appeal. Between 1950 and 1980 India achieved an annual average growth rate of 3.5 per cent, later derisively dismissed as the 'Hindu rate of growth', but an economic breakthrough of sorts when compared to the colonial era. In the first two decades of independence, state-led and tariff-protected industrialization nurtured a growing industrial bourgeoisie. Land reform, though limited to the abolition of the *latifundia*-like Zamindari system, created an aspiring—and numerically important—agrarian-capitalist class. The Congress electoral base of Dalits, tribals and mostly poor Muslims saw, or could hope to see, some improvement in their lives. This was accompanied by the institutionalization of local representative bodies, with election to office at various levels, and the subsequent linguistic division of states in 1956, all of which had some degree of public support and helped to stave off mass discontent and buy time. But the uneven outcome of development was also one of the main reasons for the erosion of Congress hegemony. By 1967 it was clear that the Nehruvian promise to bring about a social-democratic version of sustained capitalist progress had failed. The absence of more serious land redistribution ensured that mass immiseration in the countryside would continue. Growing discontent among the new agrarian-capitalist layers, and greater awareness of their mobilizing capacity at provincial level, led to them severing their earlier links with the Congress to set up their own regional parties. Statist developmentalism continued to enjoy widespread hegemony, however, backed by both the Sangh and the CPI.

At the same time, the 'winner-takes-all' electoral system established by the Constitution of India, on the Westminster model, continued to give Congress huge parliamentary majorities even as its share of the popular vote began to fall.[8] Mocking the principle of faithful representation, the first-past-the-post system gives the winning party stronger control over government and its resources, which it can then use to buy further popularity—an artificially enhanced form of hegemony. It has served the BJP equally well: in 2014, the party won 51 per cent of seats with 31 per cent of the vote and in 2019, 56 per cent of seats with 37 per cent vote share. Despite its reputation as an outstanding, liberal and democratic text, the Constitution also set family law—marriage, divorce, adoption, inheritance, family property—under the control of the various religious authorities, instead of instituting a uniform civil code. This was due in part to Congress's wooing of the Muslim Ulama for its vote block, but also to the 'soft' Hindu nationalism of so many of the Congress representatives at the 1946–50 Constituent Assembly. (Ironically, this has allowed the Sangh to position itself as more progressive than Congress, as an ardent proponent of a civil code, while castigating the other parties and secular intellectuals for seeking to 'appease' the 'backward' Muslims.). The Sangh's real aim, however, was revealed by its legislation on triple talaq which was pushed through by a majority in both Houses of Parliament in June/July 2019.[9] Having achieved this, the BJP is not going to seriously push for a fully gender-just Uniform Civil Code (UCC) since that would mean addressing some patriarchal biases in existing Hindu laws and practices concerning marriage, divorce, succession and matrimonial property as well as doing away with the Hindu Undivided Family wherein tax savings are split and the tax outgo minimised.

Insofar as the construction of hegemony requires the friction of a 'dangerous other', did the Communists Party of India serve this purpose? Certainly, during the Nehruvian era, the then-undivided CPI was the main domestic challenger, the runner-up in the first three general elections.[10] Its prestige among working masses was high; it led major industrial struggles in Bombay and powerful peasant movements in West Bengal, Bihar and Telangana, where it had sparked a major uprising in 1946 against the Nizam of Hyderabad and his landlord supporters before Nehru sent the Indian Army to seize the province, eventually accomplished at the price of a terrible pogrom.[11] In 1957 the CPI became the first opposition party to win control of a state assembly, Kerala, where it instituted land, labour and education reforms. Nehru responded by dismissing the CPI state government in 1959, a clear abuse of his legislative power. However, Moscow also put pressure on the CPI to lessen its opposition to the Congress, in support of the USSR's narrow diplomatic interests–one reason why Nehru assiduously cultivated the Soviet Union's friendship. The USSR supported Nehru's non-aligned foreign policy and also helped India set up major public-sector heavy industries. By 1962, the CPI leadership had swung round to supporting Nehru in his aggressive handling of the border conflict with China, which led to the Sino-Indian war. But this marked a major split in the Party in 1964, with the breakaway Communist Party of India (Marxist), or CPI-M, distancing itself as a sharper critic of Congress from the left, while cultivating friendlier relations with China. The smaller CPI remained so close to Congress that it actually supported Indira Gandhi's Emergency rule.

Leadership and Intelligentsia

Congress hegemony in the 1950s and 60s could also rely on the support of the intelligentsia and the media. Radio was in government hands, but even the privately owned print media were overwhelming supportive of the Nehruvian project of nation-making in this period. Nehru's persona as an educated patrician undoubtedly played a role in this: from an enormously wealthy Hindu family, schooled at Harrow, with a Cambridge degree in natural sciences, legal training at the Inner Temple and political education through the Fabian Society, he was a bestselling author of poetic volumes on Indian culture and history. But his international travels counted too. For a domestic audience, India's global status as a nation was identified with Nehru's personal credibility as a world statesman, as the main proponent of non-alignment and its most articulate propagandist. All this greatly burnished his appeal among the fledgling Indian intelligentsia, ensuring its loyalty–and, of course, guaranteeing his primacy within the party at home.[12] Nehru's extensive use of Parliament as a national platform, which he took very seriously, helped to create an aura of respect for the legislative process and parliamentary debate, the basis for a broader democratic ethos.

Arguably, the very incoherence of Congress ideology meant greater reliance on Nehru's role as a charismatic leader. Unlike the BJP and earlier political instruments of the Sangh, Congress was never a cadre-based party: Ambedkar memorably described it as a party 'open to all fools and knaves, friends and foes, communalists and secularists, reformers and orthodox, and capitalists and anti-capitalists.'[13] Organizationally, Congress was run from the apex by Sardar Patel, the party strongman, who selected and financed candidates, raised funds and cracked down on dissent. Patel represented the dominant current within the Congress leadership: upper caste and upper class, ideologically pro-Hindu (though in a softer variant than Hindutva) and economically elitist. It was Patel's early death in 1950 that gave Nehru a freer rein within the party, not necessarily because its middle and upper echelons shared the Fabian aspects of his 'idea of India'. Beyond this, what held Congress together as a powerful political force, despite rising factionalism, were its links to rural elites, the financial support of big and aspiring industrialists, and an organizational structure that could act as a network of patronage and clientelism, providing the loaves and fishes of office to leaders at various levels who, in turn, would rev up the machinery of voter mobilization at election time. It was also the only body that could carry out the hegemon's tasks of class conciliation and arbitration, hammering out policy compromises that lower castes and classes would accept. But the price paid by dependence, first upon Nehru, then his descendants, to provide a face for this machine would be a high one, as dynastic rot set in: Indira (authoritarian), Sanjay (vicious), Rajiv (corrupt), Sonia (secretive), Rahul (vacillating). The Nehru-Gandhi family's right to rule would become a dead weight on the party.

A Hinduized State Apparatus

As in Gramsci's classic formula, consent was backed with coercion in the operation of Congress hegemony. This was apparent both in the role of armed force in the construction of a 'strong', unitary Indian nation-state, at the moment of independence, and in the bloody suppression of minority, ethnic, religious and class rebellions that followed. The Partition agreement stitched up between V.P. Menon, Mountbatten, Nehru, Patel and Jinnah was pushed through at point-blank notice without popular consultation: provinces were issued with an ultimatum and their legislative assemblies told to choose between joining Congress-ruled India, Muslim League-led Pakistan or–as with Bengal and Punjab–splitting themselves between the two. At least a million were killed in the resulting panic, above all in the Punjab, and 12–18 million fled their homes. In Kashmir, an obsession of Nehru, Indian forces were air-lifted to Srinagar and took possession of most of the Muslim majority province, the Nehru government denying the promised plebiscite to ascertain the popular will.[14] Nehru and Patel also suppressed a report of the 1948 massacres in Hyderabad, where between 27,000 and 40,000 Muslims were killed when Indian troops sent in to secure the principality joined local Hindu police and armed gangs in a pogrom.[15] In Bengal, Congress–and G.D. Birla, Gandhi's millionaire patron–backed the Sangh/Hindu Mahasabha campaign for Partition against a joint Hindu-Muslim movement for a united, independent state. If these moves were largely rational, given the Congress goal of a 'strong India' characterized by Hindu predominance, Nehruvian foreign policy was more erratic. The solidaristic goals of non-alignment were abandoned when New Delhi provoked the border war with China in 1962, resulting in a humiliating defeat. Congress's nationalist and militarist *amour propre* was restored by war with Pakistan in 1965, when India escalated hostilities in response to Pakistani infiltration across the Kashmir ceasefire line.

Before Partition, Muslims made up 32 per cent of the Indian Army. After it, though the Republic of India inherited the vast bulk of the Raj's military personnel and hardware, Muslims fell to around 2 per cent. The Congress in all its years of rule did nothing to alter this demographic. The Indian military has always viewed Pakistan as its main enemy; its Hindu composition has helped to promote a conflation of sorts between anti-Pakistani and anti-Muslim sentiment, running in both directions. The then-Socialist George Fernandes, later a defence minister in the BJP coalition, summed up the position in 1985: 'The Muslim is not wanted in the Armed Forces because he is always suspect'–'whether we want to admit it or not, most Indians consider Muslims a fifth column for Pakistan.'[16] It is reasonable to assume that a significant proportion of officers and soldiers have long been sympathetic to Hindutva. In the late 1980s and early 90s, during the 'Rama's Birthplace' campaign–the Ram Janmabhoomi, in which right-wing Hindu groups fought to build a temple on the site of the old Babri Masjid in Ayodhya, Uttar Pradesh, claiming the mosque was located where the god had been born–Indian Army chiefs made clear they would not take responsibility for protecting the mosque because Army *jawans* were overwhelmingly Hindus whose battle cries were invocations of Lord Ram. (The Indian Army exhibited no such qualms when it came to military assaults on the Sikhs' Golden Temple in 1984 or the Muslim shrine of Charar-e-Sharif in Kashmir in 1995 to capture or kill respectively Sikh and Islamic separatists. Both events took place under Congress rule.[17]).

A similar mindset prevailed in other agencies of the coercive state. The central intelligence agencies set up by Congress–the Intelligence Bureau (IB) in 1947, the Central Board of Investigation (CBI) in 1963, the Research and Analysis Wing (RAW) in 1968–have never had an independent legal framework or Charter of Duties to safeguard against political manipulation; the IB has carried out election analyses and forecasts for the governing party. Another body, the National Investigation Agency (NIA) was set up in 2008, under a Congress-led government, to deal with 'terrorism'; to date its targets have included journalists and stone-throwing teenagers in Kashmir, as well as Naxalite militants.

The Hindu communalization of the police has been particularly frightening. Constitutionally the state governments have had responsibility for maintaining law and order, unless they called for help from the Centre. But state police were poorly trained, ill-disciplined and under-equipped compared to the Indian Police Service (IPS), which answered to the central government. Technically the IPS was supposed to make law-enforcement decisions independently of governing parties during demonstrations, strikes, elections, riots–but governments wielded the power of postings and transfers over recalcitrant officers.[18] Communal attitudes have been pervasive. Several official inquiries, including by the National Police Commission, have shown police partiality in acting as a 'Hindu force', with perceptible discrimination against Muslims in the use of violence, preventive arrests, curfew decisions and treatment of detainees.[19] In communal riots, Hindus see the police as friends and protectors; not so Muslims. All too often, police actively collaborate with the rioters.[20] As a result, Muslims, the principal sufferers in riots, actually ask for Army intervention, not trusting the partisan police and paramilitaries.

2. Hegemony of the BJP

What are the similarities and contrasts between this Nehruvian mode of rule and that of today's BJP? Some continuities have already been noted. As with Congress at its height, Modi's parliamentary dominance is based on first-past-the-post pluralities in the densely populated 'cow belt' states of the Hindi heartland, where–unlike in the South, which had strong anti-Brahmin movements–Brahminized and upper-caste values, attitudes and practices have held wider and deeper cultural-ideological sway.[21] This concentration of support in the populous, seat-rich states of the North and West explains why the BJP could secure a single-party majority in 2014 with only 31 per cent of the overall vote: the BJP won 131 of the 149 seats in Uttar Pradesh, Madhya Pradesh and Bihar.[22] At the same time, it is reasonable to believe that both former Congress voters and supporters of regional parties switched to the BJP, suggesting that Hindutva has become an attractive worldview especially among youth and an aspirational category of voters categorized as 'not rich, not middle class, not below the poverty line'.[23] No solace can be taken from the BJP's relatively low percentage of the vote in 2014. Between 2014 and 2019 it secured single-party rule in sixteen of twenty-nine states, with four others ruled through coalition partners. (Congress at its peak controlled eighteen states.). In 2019 not only did the BJP's vote share rise by six percentage points but as in 2014 the voter turnout by youth was higher than the overall rate and the BJP on both occasions won the largest single vote share among 18-22 year olds.

Ideologically, the Sangh's call to 'make India strong' represents a coarser more belligerent and exclusivist nationalism than the Congress brand. The contrast with what China had achieved domestically, as well its rising global status, could only fuel the sense of relative inferiority. In the eyes of the BJP's new layer of elite supporters, Congress had failed to build a nation that–by virtue of its size, population, resources and a past history of civilizational attainment beyond anything that the West had achieved–deserved nothing less. The Indian nation must no longer be weakened by 'culprits' from within or without. As a hegemonic ideology, the BJP/Sangh's harder form of Hindu nationalism is better equipped to call for subordination to a 'higher cause' and thereby achieve a working reconciliation of competing interests.

Party and Leader

The most obvious contrasts with Congress lie in the organizational character of the BJP and the figure of its national leader. One striking difference with almost all the other parties, including the Congress and the Left, is that the BJP has never suffered a major split—testament to its ideological discipline and cohesion. The party operates a streamlined hierarchy, where each level takes decisions about the level below and obeys the one above it. Amit Shah, when party president in Modi's first term, positioned himself and his coterie at the apex of states having forthcoming assembly elections. Below this apex come district chiefs, then block heads and so on, down to units which comprise 12 booth committees. These committees provide information on local caste composition, to help target appropriate messaging and election-day mobilization. The BJP also poaches many 'likely-to-win' candidates from local parties that are not opposed in principle to Sangh ideology, tempting them through lure of money, re-election promises and the fact of having such a powerful voter-mobilizing capacity.[24] But the BJP's biggest asset remains its massive cadre base, which includes foot soldiers willing to wreak violence on command. The rise of the far right is a worldwide phenomenon, but nowhere else is there a force like the Sangh, which has had an unbroken existence of over ninety years and a width and depth of implantation in civil society unmatched in any other country. The BJP and the Sangh, the broader family to which it belongs, represent a far-right force with undeniable neo-fascist characteristics. Apart from the BJP and RSS, the VHP (World Hindu Council) founded in 1964 is the other main pan-Indian body. It is the 'overlord' for cultural-religious activities, with mutually beneficial links to the leaders of numerous Hindu sects. VHP muscle and money help these sects to grow, thereby enhancing the aura of their leaders, who duly call on their devotees to support Sangh campaigns, programmes and electoral candidates.[25]

The RSS has around three dozen affiliates, ranging from associations of ex-servicemen, scientists, accountants, etc., to one of the largest trade-union federations, a peasant organization, a women's organization and the biggest student wing. It has the country's largest network of private schools, the Vidya Bharati and close to eight hundred NGOs working in areas of disaster relief, health and development.[26] The RSS now has over 58,000 local branches (*shakas*) which hold daily, weekly and monthly meetings for their members, differentiated by age, profession and motivational levels.[27] All this is held together by seasoned RSS and VHP cadres, full- and part-time, who are regularly accountable to their superiors. Decades of such routinized welfare and mobilizing activities explain why Hindutva has expanded outside the Hindi heartland into parts of the northeast, the south and one-time left strongholds like Tripura, West Bengal and Kerala. Being in power at the Centre and in so many states means the Sangh now attracts many more supporters by straightforward patronage politics, while retaining an expanded core of the ideological faithful.

While caste remains important in shaping voter preferences, the personalization of politics is also a fact. Opinion polls consistently show Modi to be significantly more popular than the BJP or RSS, let alone other party leaders. As their political front-man, Modi could hardly be a starker contrast to the Congress dynasts. Born in 1950, he comes from a modest background in small-town Gujarat–his father ran a tea stall at the local railway station–and a community classed among the Other Backward Castes (OBCs). He began attending RSS sessions while still a child. At eighteen he quit his family home and his new bride, Jashodaben–the marriage had been contracted when they were both children–apparently aiming to enter an ashram, but was rejected for his lack of higher education. Settling in Ahmedabad, Modi worked his way up through the ranks of the Gujarati RSS as a full-time militant, going underground during the Emergency. In 1985 he was assigned to electoral organizing for the BJP, becoming national secretary of the party in 1995 and helping to secure its electoral victory of 1999. Rather than serve in the national government under Vajpayee and Advani, however, Modi edged out the incumbent BJP Chief Minister in Gujarat to take the job himself.

Modi's personal ruthlessness was apparent in the way he treated his abandoned wife, who was denied a passport by his government.

Ironically, this very absence of close family ties has given him the public aura of a dedicated patriot with no reason to be personally corrupt.[28] Modi has always followed a health and yoga regimen that gives him remarkable physical energy to devote to politics throughout the day and much of the night. He is a skilled public orator in Hindi and Gujarati, but dislikes critical or sophisticated interlocutors and avoids Parliament, where he has never subjected himself to open question-and-answer sessions. Compared to Nehru or Indira Gandhi, Modi has a rigid and inflexible mind for which the prescriptions of Hindutva *are* the truth. The media are kept at arms' length: favoured journalists are allowed the rare newspaper or TV interview. Modi is the only Indian prime minister who, in his first term never held a public press conference. This is a pattern very likely to be repeated during his second stint as PM. Yet never before has any Indian leader plastered billboards, bus-stands, newspapers—everywhere—with his own image, topping government proclamations of all kinds, even stooping to take pictorial credit for the smallest government schemes initiated by this or that ministry, including programmes set up under the previous administrations. Either Modi's self-obsession knows no bounds, or he thinks that a Goebbelsian construction of personalized populism is basic to the recipe for political longevity. Nor has any prime minister been quite so peripatetic. By the autumn of 2019, he had visited 60 countries in six continents. This apparently has less to do with compelling geo-political and economic considerations than with the drive of an insecure personality to project oneself as a world leader.

The Prime Minister's Office today is highly secretive and power is tightly centralized, even if Modi doesn't quite enjoy the solitary pre-eminence of Nehru. On domestic affairs, the two who count are Modi and Amit Shah, the former party president now the home minister in the new Union Cabinet reinforcing his earlier status as already the second most powerful person in the country.[29] On foreign policy Modi relies on Ajit Doval, a former Intelligence Bureau chief with a record of skullduggery in the North-East, Myanmar and Kashmir and on Subrahmanyam Jaishankar, the newly appointed foreign minister. Jaishankar has been a career diplomat who served as a faithful and obedient foreign secretary in Modi's first term and whose understanding of the global order has never extended beyond the crudities of standardised 'national interest' *realpolitik* untainted by any moral inhibitions or by any larger vision of how to properly address increasingly transnational dilemmas of economics, politics and the environment. The bond between Shah and Modi is based on their division of responsibilities and the fact that each knows too much about the other to risk undermining him. This personalization of power by Modi is not something that the RSS entirely approves of–the organization is all. But recognizing that state power is crucial for its Hindutva project, which has allowed the BJP to gain more ground in the relationship between the two, the RSS has had to stay quiet. However, should Modi's personal popularity falter–economic problems, electoral losses–the knives could be out with Shah waiting in the wings to take over.

Media and Intelligentsia

The Modi government doesn't enjoy the same monopoly of media support as the Congress at its height. Nevertheless, it has benefited from the dramatic expansion in vernacular newspapers and non-English TV channels since the mid-80s. In the north, centre and west of India, the dominant print and electronic media are in Hindi and, by virtue of their upper-caste ownership, broadly aligned to 'Hindu politics'. English-language papers and TV channels traditionally tilted more to Congress and, as the 'Brahmins' of the media world, had an influence far greater than their circulation and viewing figures would otherwise warrant. This has changed, thanks to two key shifts in power relations. Journalists are now mostly on short-term contracts, as elsewhere, and are more beholden to the political whims and monetary preoccupations of proprietors and management, who have in turn subordinated themselves more fully to political authority. Advertising from government-controlled units at the state and central levels constitutes an important source of revenues for them. The BJP government is less bothered than the Congress about presenting a liberal face, and seems even more determined to micro-monitor and quietly warn papers and channels about allowing 'excessive' criticism, retracting financial support from those who disobey. Both the Press Council of India, which is supposed to play an independent watchdog role, and the body responsible for the accreditation of journalists, are now saturated with BJP appointees. The 'Murdochization' of much of the print and electronic media is a fact.[30] In the US, where historically the growth of corporations was more independent of Central power and largesse, the corporate-controlled media have been much more critical of Trump than their Indian counterparts have dared to be of Modi.

The RSS/BJP caught on to social media much earlier than the Congress–the BJP set up a website in 1995, the Congress in 2003. Modi had Facebook and Twitter accounts in 2009, and now has personalized accounts as prime minister, with over 50 million Twitter followers, the highest of any world political leader; Congress President Rahul has 6 million.[31] The RSS helped the BJP to set up a huge social-media cell with its own branches for organized trolling. According to a disillusioned former insider this is superbly organized, with paid techies given hit-lists of people to attack and going into overdrive during elections. Apparently there are no legal financial limits on party-political propaganda on social media.[32] It is something of an irony that, compared to print, TV and radio–where Modi has his own monthly talk show on the state broadcasting channels–counter-propaganda against the BJP can be done very cheaply on social media.

Interestingly, over the past fifteen years the BJP/Sangh has acquired what the Congress always possessed, namely a substantial layer of articulate, English-speaking commentators, policy experts and ideologues. How and why did this come about? It built on part on the existing Hindu 'common sense' about the Hindu-Muslim relationship, in conditions where a 'fuzzy' identity boundary, which had persisted through centuries of coexistence–basically a functional one, of work and exchange–had been sharpened by Partition. Given the appropriate circumstances, past and present prejudices could more easily translate into the belligerent nationalism of the Hindu *rashtra*, or nation–which would have been far more difficult to believe in, let alone try and bring about, had the country not been partitioned, with half its Muslim population hived off to Pakistan. The key fact is that this layer of the intelligentsia has accepted the Sangh version of what is required to 'make India strong'. At the same time, a number of prominent liberal intellectuals who cautiously welcomed Modi's ascent in 2014, believing that the demands of government would moderate BJP behaviour, have now become opponents, dismayed by Modi's disregard for their 'vision of India'. A more general climate of fear, plus higher levels of public abuse and legal harassment of dissenters and liberal NGOs, has promoted greater self-censorship and political conformism, however reluctant.

Hegemonizing public culture and education has always been the Sangh goal. In the coalition governments of 1977-80 and 1998-2004, its leaders fought hard for control over the Information and Broadcasting (I & B) and Human Resource Development (HRD) ministries. Now ruling on its own, the BJP has moved further and faster in appointing its people at the head of national and state universities, research centres, technical institutes, school textbook committees, cultural academies, archives, censorship boards and so forth. Congress, of course, sought to block the appointment of independent-minded Marxists to these bodies in the 1950s and 60s, but that process usually operated behind the scenes, relying on a widely shared establishment outlook, without requiring active political intervention. Today, overt manipulation–or flagrant disregard of existing rules–to plant ideologically loyal teaching staff in national universities has reached new heights. Jawaharlal Nehru University (JNU)–whose Social Science and Humanities faculties had become the main training ground for home-grown liberal and leftist intellectuals–has suffered serious setbacks from a centrally approved onslaught on its standards of recruitment, research and teaching, despite the courageous resistance of many teachers and students. The BJP also aims to replace (even as it suborns) the University Grants Commission, charged with national oversight of over 800 universities and 40,000 colleges. A new Higher Education Commission, controlled by central government, will focus on establishing 'uniform' academic standards—codeword for the Hindutva agenda. Failure to meet them will incur penalties, while new courses will require prior authorization. Meanwhile funding cuts will push public institutions towards privatization.[33] By comparison, Congress manipulation in higher education was more haphazard and delimited.

Continuing Coercion

Both Congress and the BJP have sought to crush the Maoist insurgency—Manmohan Singh, the last Congress prime minister, called it, not Hindutva, the gravest threat to internal security. Similarly, in Kashmir and the North-East, the BJP has continued the programme of repression it inherited from Congress, aimed at maintaining political control and territorial unity no matter the human cost. To this the BJP has added an extra ideological overlay of hatred for Muslims and ramped up the Congress boasts of 'teaching Pakistan a lesson'. Hence the Modi government's deliberate publicizing of the routine incursions and cross-border shooting in which both sides have long engaged. This is a deliberate gambit to rouse public anger domestically and to present the forces of Hindutva as the most determined protectors of national pride and honour. Naturally it is the Muslim inhabitants of the Kashmir Valley who suffer the most, with the youth particular targets of the Indian security forces. Congress under Nehru had already brought in quasi-colonial laws granting immunity to armed personnel in these regions, no matter how viciously or high-handedly they behaved towards the people there. But On August 5, 2019 the re-elected BJP government through an unconstitutional and illegal Presidential Order annulled Article 370 which had guaranteed Kashmir an enduring autonomous status.[34] In the days preceding and the weeks after August 5, the Central government imposed a severe military and communications lockdown including preventive arrests of Kashmiri leaders in flagrant violation of their basic human rights.

But this should have occasioned no surprise. In the last few years the Indian Army in Kashmir has stepped up its pattern of ruthless repression including the indiscriminate and mass-scale use of pellet guns, firing into the faces of protesters and bystanders alike, with thousands partially or wholly blinded and otherwise disfigured. The military has also been firing live bullets against protesting citizens and stone-throwers, the latter routinely designated as allies of 'terrorists' and therefore justifiably targeted in a ruthless and inhuman manner. The Army top brass has been emboldened in voicing its political biases. The former Army Chief of Staff, General Bipin Rawat (now made the country's first ever Chief of Defence Staff or CDS), has earlier thundered that a predominantly Muslim body in Assam, the All-India United Democratic Front (AIUDF), has been growing faster than the BJP by virtue of 'planned immigration' from Bangladesh. Gen. V.K. Singh, who in Modi's first term was the junior Minister of State for Defence and a former Army Chief of Staff, joined the BJP a few years after retiring from the Army, and donned the full uniform of the RSS when he was invited to one of its functions.[35]

Communal riots have been a recurrent feature in India under state governments of all colours, except for those of the Left. The overwhelming bulk of victims have been Muslim. So far none has surpassed in scale the 1948 massacres in Hyderabad. The 2002 pogrom in Gujarat, however, set two new precedents. For the first time, there were widespread attacks on Muslims in numerous villages, and large numbers of Dalits, Adivasis and women took part. This pattern has been subsequently repeated. These are not random outbreaks of violence but assaults that are politically determined by the Sangh in their timing and purpose. Psychologically speaking, the involvement of otherwise subordinate and marginal sections of the population like women, Dalits and Adivasis has proved to be a debased form of 'empowerment', serving to highlight Hindu-Muslim identities while masking caste and gender differences through the collective practice of violence. Episodic riots on this scale require a trigger and some degree of prior preparation. In the last five years they have been complemented by routinized, micro-level attacks on individual Muslims by groups of 'outraged Hindus' in the name of cow protection, or suspicion of being illegal migrants, or other concocted reasons, including simply being a Muslim.[36] Perpetrators mostly get away without being charged, while senior leaders involved in large-scale riots have now been reprieved.[37] The result is a wider sense of insecurity among Muslims because of the banalization of everyday violence. The propaganda success lies not so much in Hindus hating Muslims—a majority are probably indifferent to their plight—but in labelling talk of the Muslim condition today as 'minority appeasement' that diverts attention from the problems of the Hindu majority.

Institutions

Given that the 'common sense' worldview of the Indian Armed Forces (despite the fact that its formal rules of behaviour are supposed to be secular) and of the Police has long been a harder variant of Hindu nationalism, what about the other national institutions? The Indian Civil Service was trained from the start to obey its political masters. Ideologically, for the Sangh, the more committed senior bureaucrats are to Hindutva the better: there is now an official proposal to allow lateral entry to top administrative positions by government-selected outsiders. That the top three constitutional posts—prime minister, president, vice-president, with all their associated powers—are now all headed by former cadre of the RSS, certainly helps. Beyond this, the Modi government has its eye on the two bodies that have hitherto been the most independent from the executive: the Election Commission—officials who travel round the country at election times, organizing and overseeing the voting processes, state by state—and the judiciary. For the first, the BJP in 2018 introduced electoral 'bonds' which big donors can purchase for political funding. The names and sums involved would be kept secret, known only to select branches of the biggest public sector State Bank of India that created the bonds—and therefore to the government—and so a huge boost for money power in elections. In the 2019 general elections, of the funding received by parties through this route, the BJP got an estimated 95 per cent.[38]

India's reputation as the 'world's largest democracy' is highly disputable: its macro-electoral structures have endured but are substantially hollowed out and, in any case, produce gross first-past-the-post distortions of the popular will; at the meso- and micro-level there is so much violence that the label 'respecting the democratic rights of the people' hardly seems deserved. However, despite instances of booth capturing and manipulation of electronic-voting machines since their recent introduction, one crucial aspect of democratic functioning is that there really has been no reason to dispute final outcomes in general and state elections, even if victory margins may be questionable. Both BJP and Congress, with all the resources of incumbency, and confident of returning to power, have suffered unanticipated defeats at election times. This is a tribute to the Election Commissions of the past. Whether such neutral regulation by the EC, at least in regard to vote-counting, will last remains to be seen.

Clearly, the BJP has no intention of dispensing with the electoral system. That the party is investing so much effort in building up its formidable vote-mobilizing machinery, that Modi spends so much more time than any previous prime minister on the campaign trail, and so much energy goes into data mining to back up direct messaging through social media and face-to-face canvassing, should be evidence of that. The BJP wants the legitimacy provided by winning power through elections, and it is unlikely that Modi will impose a period of 'emergency rule' to match Indira's. The aim is not to eradicate this key dimension of a liberal-democratic set-up but to continue to exploit the legitimating ideal of 'majority rule' as the basis for building a Hindu *rashtra* in which 'Hindu interests' are prioritized. In this view minorities, Muslims in particular, must either accept the fact that they live in a 'Hindu India'—all the stronger as a nation, culturally and politically, for being so—or face the consequences.

Over the past fifty years India's Supreme Court has all too often prostrated itself before government dictates and pressures. By contrast to the American system, which gives state-level high courts much greater independence in resisting Supreme Court rulings—currently allowing a significant degree of legal fightback against Trump's directives—India's Supreme Court is one of the most powerful in the world and simply overrules state courts, for better and worse. As a result, the Executive doesn't have to worry much about lower courts; the apex of the system is the key target. Utterly supine during Congress Emergency rule in the seventies, the Supreme Court stiffened its spine somewhat in the eighties, but from the nineties has largely conformed to the perspectives of the regime in power at the Centre, especially with respect to communal issues such as the 1992 demolition of the Babri Masjid. The perpetrators of the illegal and criminal placement of Hindu idols in 1949 in what was a functioning Babri Mosque have never been punished nor the idols removed. Instead worship inside by Muslims was unjustly denied, and to appear even-handed the gates to the inner sanctum were locked to deny Hindu worshippers. But crucially, the idols themselves were not removed as they should have been. After the mosque destruction in 1992, the restoration of the area to the mosque's rightful owners, the Sunni Wakf Board, was first delayed and then abrogated when an Allahabad High Court ruled that it should be partitioned between three claimants, two of them Hindu. That ruling then came before the Supreme Court for final adjudication; a former Chief Justice, J.S. Khehar, had actually suggested that he mediate an out-of-court settlement between victim and victimizers. The former Chief Justice Ranjan Gogoi was head of a bench ruling on this issue in unprecedented daily sessions and was determined to bring out a final verdict before his retirement on November 17, 2019. Such is the political reality today that it was no surprise when on November 9, 2019, the SC to its eternal discredit, in a five-judge Constitutional bench gave a unanimous verdict handing over the whole site to the key Hindu claimant to allow the Ram Mandir to be built where the Sangh wants it. Those who have endorsed and benefited from the criminal illegalities involved in desecrating and then destroying the mosque have been rewarded!

The Supreme Court has proved only somewhat tougher in defending its own privileges. So far it has opposed attempts by both Congress and BJP governments to give the Executive formal veto power over the appointment of top-ranking judges, whose selection is reserved to the Collegium of the Supreme Court. But in practice it has largely acceded to Executive wishes. In 2017, the Modi government negotiated the right to veto an appointment on grounds of 'national security', on the basis of a written objection. It has succeeded in getting the Supreme Court and all High Courts to compile databases on judges and now supposedly 'assists' in making appointments, although this had been stalled because the Centre during the tenure of the former Chief Justice Dipak Misra (August 28, 2017 to October 2, 2018) still did not approve the Memorandum of Procedure detailing the administrative process for appointments. Misra, was accused of acquiring land under a false affidavit when he was a lawyer and of failing to recuse himself in a Supreme Court case in which he'd earlier been involved–instead ruling in favour of two High Court judges under investigation for possible bribery.[39] In January 2018, the next four top-ranking judges had held a press conference criticizing Misra for failing to address their grievances, particularly regarding his allocation of sensitive cases to lower-ranking judges, in disregard of seniority or expertise, and in violation of past norms and procedures. The implication was that Misra was accommodating Shah and Modi's desires; his record as judge and lawyer would certainly make him vulnerable to such pressures. This Supreme Court, then, is the frail safeguard of rights–and the source for any legal resistance, admittedly far from resolute, to Hindutva. Against the Modi government, it has for the first time explicitly read privacy as a fundamental right. It continues to be the only interpreter of the 'basic structure' of the Constitution, which means it can be an obstacle to Sangh efforts to endowing Hinduism with a special status in the Constitution, whether or not the word 'secular' is removed from the Preamble. But if the SC does not revoke the annulment of Article 370 on Kashmir or the unprecedented downgrading (and bifurcation) of J&K from statehood to that of two separate Union Territories of J&K and Ladakh, then it will be a clear signal that the SC is not now or in the future going to be as 'independent' an arbiter, as it is empowered to be, of what the Constitution basically stands for.

In sum: there are some striking similarities between the two hegemonies. Both have drawn their support from the powerful states of the Hindi heartland, amplified by the first-past-the-post electoral system. Both dominate the national-political landscape, facing no rival party of the same order—unlike the two-party system in the US, for example. Both have charismatic leaders, who claim a special right to lead India—Nehru, through his role in the independence movement and social status; Modi, through his seemingly patriotic devotion to the cause of making India strong. For both, the principal enemies have been China and Pakistan. Both have used crushing force to impose national control over rebellious border regions. Both have, on occasion, permitted pogroms against Muslims to go unpunished. The two hegemons have each exploited the intelligence services and the judiciary for their own political ends. Both have had close ties to big capital. Both have been fêted in the West. Yet there are strong contrasts between them too—divergences both in style and in epoch. At leadership level, the aristocratic, Anglophone, jet-setting Nehru-Gandhi dynasty are worlds away from the plebeian piety of Modi, most at ease speaking Hindi or Gujarati. For mediating mechanisms and voter turnout, Congress relied on traditional relations of deference and dependence, especially in the countryside; the BJP, on cadre mobilization, social media and a lumpen-aspirational OBC social base. The use of religious ideology by Congress was latent; by the BJP, aggressive and overt. Other differences speak to the changing times. The main domestic enemy for Congress was communism; for the BJP, Islam. Nehruvian foreign policy was premised on (qualified) non-alignment, Modi's on close alliance with the US against China.

3. Dynamics of the Interregnum

What features of the long interregnum after Congress fed into the rise of the BJP? Two stand out. First, the failure of Congress developmentalism to lift mass living standards—the damning evidence of the Congress record on literacy and primary healthcare in the villages, as well as water, sanitation, electrification, roads—

and the step-by-step shift to increasingly neoliberal policies as a solution, produced major social tensions for which Congress could offer no persuasive hegemonic formula. In other words, Congress introduced the upheaval but proved incapable of managing the turmoil that resulted among different fractions of capital–one of the key tasks of a capitalist hegemon. The decade of the 1980s proved critical.[40] Returned to office after the collapse of the 1977–79 Janata coalition that followed the Emergency, Indira Gandhi–and even more so her son Rajiv, after her assassination in 1984–turned from dirigisme to deregulation (for domestic and international capital) and repression (for labour). In successive moves, Congress lifted capital restrictions, pushed through the 'de-licensing' of the public sector to enable penetration by private capital, introduced tax concessions for business and higher-income brackets, freed up imports of machinery and consumer goods, cut subsidies for public-distribution schemes and brought in laws to crack down on strikes, go-slows and work-to-rule protests.[41] Politically, Congress moved towards a tighter partnership with the more modern, export-oriented sectors of big business that could compete more successfully in the de-regulated environment it was creating.

A Post-statist Vacuum

Socially, however, capital-intensive investment meant lower employment absorption and rising inequalities, leading to greater frustrations below. Agrarian capital, especially in the south and west, felt abandoned by Congress, while the businesses that had benefited most from import-substituting industrialization fretted about the influx of cheap foreign goods. These multi-layered discontents emerged into the ideological vacuum that followed the death of the developmentalist Nehruvian Consensus. The political outcomes were therefore uneven. Initially, the biggest beneficiaries of Congress's electoral decline were regional forces, backed by huge agricultural lobbies, where the rich farmers came largely, though not exclusively, from the upper non-Brahmin castes and higher echelons of the OBCs, supported by a much larger stratum of aspiring middle peasants from lower OBC ranks. Agrarian capital, actual and aspiring, sought to use its ability to mobilize mass-voter support to leverage provincial governments to enhance its relative power vis-a-vis industrial and urban-based capital. This was the short-lived period of 'Bharat'–the Hindi word for India–versus 'India'.[42]

At the time, many saw the decline of the Congress as ushering in a 'second democratic upsurge', a kind of coming-of-age with the third generation after independence. The new-found assertiveness of lower and 'other backward castes', along with the emergence of regional Dalit parties, was clearly a democratic development in a country that had been governed since independence by a Brahmin family from Uttar Pradesh. India's immense diversity would now be expressed in the 'regionalization' of even national-level politics, making the Centre more responsive to public needs throughout the country, even if the price to be paid for this was an inevitable run of short-lived coalition governments. What this optimistic viewpoint failed to see was, first, how the politics of caste-identity assertion could promote harder variants of Hindu nationalism; and second, the extent to which socio-economic tensions and discontents were creating fertile political ground for the BJP/Sangh.

Indira Gandhi, on her return in the early 80s from the post-Emergency wilderness, had encouraged RSS and Sangh followers to support her, thus widening her electoral base, at a time when she was opposing Sikh separatist militancy and the Jan Sangh was remodelling itself as the BJP. After her assassination and in the election of 1984 that immediately followed, her son Rajiv won by a landslide. Being the result of a sudden unpredictable sympathy wave he understood that this Congress support was only temporary and brittle and therefore he attempted to garner mass support by playing the twin religious cards of appeasing both Hindu and Muslim communal forces. First he upheld Muslim Personal Law, enacting legislation in 1986 to overturn the Supreme Court verdict mandating husbands to provide maintenance for wives they had divorced. Then, to counter charges of 'Muslim appeasement', he ordered the opening of the locked gates of the Babri Masjid, allowing Hindu worship of the Ram idols that had illegally been placed there in 1949. This gave a dramatic fillip to the building of the Ayodhya movement which had been initiated by the VHP in 1984 while the eruption of the Bofors scandal in 1987 played into the hands of all the opposition parties. In the second half of the eighties V.P. Singh's Janata Dal, the CPI-M (from its base in West Bengal), the BJP and others all saw their political fortunes rise as revealed in the 1989 polls. It was in this juncture that the BJP riding the growing momentum of the Ram Janmabhoomi campaign would see its Lok Sabha tally rise from only 2 seats in 1984 to 89 in 1989.[43] The Congress response to this upsurge in Hindu-nationalist militancy merely helped to pave the BJP's way.

Congress continued on the same lines after Rajiv's assassination in 1991: for fear of offending 'Hindu sentiment', Congress Prime Minister Narasimha Rao did nothing to stop the campaign that would defy the Constitution, with impunity, by demolishing the Babri Masjid in Ayodhya in 1992–demonstrating the de facto sovereignty of the forces of Hindutva in defying the law. At the same time, Congress finance minister Manmohan Singh accelerated the turn to neoliberalism citing pressure from the IMF. Market de-regulation, external liberalization, financial reform, greater capital mobility and a harsher labour regime duly followed. With Congress unable to manage the tensions this created, opportunities opened up for another potential hegemon to expand and exercise national influence.

New Pan-Hinduism

The second key factor in the interregnum period was the BJP's ability to recast itself for bourgeois rule–or the Sangh's ability to recast the BJP. Received wisdom had it that the BJP could only hope to gain national influence if it shed, or at least greatly moderated, its hard-line Hindu-nationalist ideological straitjacket, which would inevitably alienate the numerically vast lower-caste and Dalit electoral blocs. But this did not take place. Instead, the BJP succeeded in adjusting its class formula while keeping its ideological message intact–in fact, intensifying it, with a spate of religious-political processions, campaigns, pilgrimages and other forms of religiosity, mobilizing the golden chariots, warrior kings and stirring soundtrack of the *Ramayana*, in its countless film and TV versions, to calculated effect. The growing assertiveness of OBCs and Dalits did temporarily hamper the Sangh, but lessons were quickly learnt. From initially opposing positive discrimination–OBC reservations in central government jobs and education–it accepted them. Meanwhile, the Hindutva spectacles generally met with approval and often mass participation from OBC ranks. Even if they still supported their own political vehicles, often regional parties, many responded to the invitation to seek emotional uplift and cultural mobility through identification with an ever-broader Hindu community, itself being transformed into the more monolithic form that historian Romila Thapar has described as 'syndicated Hinduism'.[44] In due course, many sub-castes within the Dalits would seek similar identification as a way of achieving greater acceptance and appreciation from higher castes.

The success of the BJP campaign was apparent within two short years. In 1996, the regional parties shunned the prospect of entering a coalition with the BJP–which, though the largest party in the Lok Sabha, could therefore rule for only thirteen days. By 1998 these parties had abandoned their not even skin-deep claims to secularism and joined the BJP in stitching up just such an alliance. The ongoing Hindutva-ization of OBCs then enabled the BJP to eat into the social and electoral bases of the regional parties, particularly in the northern half of the country. Simultaneously, it expanded its support among the top 15-20 per cent of the population. Corporate capital was looking for an alternative national party to protect and promote its interests, given Congress vicissitudes. If neoliberalism reflects a global trend in economic policy-making, it can only be stabilized in a given country by a corresponding shift in politics and ideology which, to be sustainable, must be made to express national specificities. Profit-making is primary: Indian capital always seeks domestic political stability. In quick time, the BJP shed its old ideological baggage of economic nationalism, with only feeble murmurs of dissent from a small section of the Sangh.

The first two BJP-led coalition governments of 1998-99 and 1999-2004, under Vajpayee, strengthened the hegemonic reach of the Sangh. Vajpayee and Advani, his Number Two, parachuted favoured bureaucrats into key positions and began the process of saffronizing the education system. Muslim madrasas were designated potential breeding-grounds for pro-Pakistani terrorists, justifying closer official scrutiny, while Sangh foot soldiers carried out scattered attacks on madrasas, dargahs and mosques. Central government resources were diverted to pro-Hindutva affiliates and NGOs. Strikingly, none of the BJP's coalition partners quit over the May 1998 nuclear tests, when Vajpayee declared India an atomic power. Except for the Left, all other parties including the Congress soon enough endorsed the bomb in the name of a stronger India. The second test came with the Gujarat pogrom of 2002: what marked this as an ideological turning-point was that none of BJP's allies, for all their mealy-mouthed criticisms, were prepared to pull the government down. The message for the Hindu supporters of these regional parties was to endorse the BJP suggestion that the Muslims may have somehow 'deserved' their fate–hence no governmental retribution against the attacking Hindu mobs–and that there was therefore implicit merit in the Sangh claim about 'Muslim appeasement' having gone far enough.

The BJP fell in 2004 not because of any disillusionment with its ideology, though some were discomfited by Gujarat, but because of its economic record–the gains of 'Shining India' going largely to the urban middle class. More important, however, was the fact that Congress could stitch together an alliance with discontented regional parties.[45] Congress-led coalitions under Manmohan Singh then reigned for two full terms, till 2014, fostering illusions about the basic incompatibility between Indian heterogeneity and Hindutva homogeneity. But one of the main reasons why Congress won again in 2009–its vote rising a modest 2 per cent, yielding an additional 61 seats–was its introduction of the world's largest 'National Rural Employment Guarantee Act'. This was thanks to combined pressure from the civil-society organizations that had drafted the legislation and the Left parties, which supported it from outside the government. However modest its impact on the ground, NREGA provided incomes (for rural women, in particular), raised average wages in the countryside and, along with road-building and other construction projects, did make some difference. After 2009, however, the momentum behind NREGA slackened. High inflation and Congress corruption helped to discredit the ruling coalition–and provided ammunition for the BJP/RSS social-media campaigns targeting the 100 million first-time voters in the 2014 elections. In September 2013, after much back-room manoeuvring with the RSS, Modi was proclaimed the BJP prime ministerial candidate, sidelining Vajpayee and Advani. His victories in May 2014 when he secured a slim single party majority and then his more comfortable expanded majority in 2019 seems to have put paid to the notion that India was developing a stable two-party system. All the more so because of the very poor electoral showing of each of the opposition parties with as many of them willing to work with the BJP in power than against it. The Congress as the single biggest opposition went from 44 seats in 2014 to 52 in 2019.

4. What Now?

The BJP/Sangh is clear about its short and long-term plans: over the next five years it hopes to consolidate its hegemony, to be–as Congress once was–the only national player around which the ruling class can coalesce. As always, the main weakness for an incumbent party in India is the state of the economy. The problems are structural and long precede Modi. Despite annual average growth of around 7 per cent, mass poverty persists and the rate of employment absorption is miserably low, while inequalities of income and wealth accumulate. Absolute poverty is around 30 per cent, but when cost assessments of basic needs like education, health care, housing and social security are taken into account, another 40 per cent fall into the category of the 'vulnerable poor', for whom the shock of a bad harvest, high inflation or a family illness can wreak havoc. The pattern has if anything worsened, mocking Modi's slogan of *acche din* [good days] coming. For perhaps the first time since independence, total employment actually fell between

2013–14 and 2015–16.[46] In November 2016, Modi's flagship policy of demonetization–500 and 1,000 rupee notes ($7 and $14) were cancelled overnight and had to be deposited at banks, in a bid to crack down on the shadow economy–succeeded for a time in raising his stock as a class warrior for the un-corrupt poor. But it also accounted in part for a continuous economic slowdown across seven quarters between January 2016 and September 2017, raising costs for farmers while their incomes stagnated, as did rural wages. Nor did the corporate sector or international capital get the concessions they wanted from Modi, such as accelerated privatizations in public-sector enterprises, including banks. In September 2019 more confident after its second victory the BJP government did significantly cut corporate tax to a maximum of 25 per cent hoping to raise 'animal spirits'. This supply side measure by seriously reducing the capacity of the government to itself invest and spend on welfare, has as its negative counterpart on the demand side the reduction of overall purchasing power. It remains doubtful that these tax cuts (which will no doubt be followed by income tax cuts in the highest brackets) will lift investment back to the level of 34 per cent of GDP that it enjoyed in 2011, from its present 27–29 per cent range.

It remains to be seen whether the BJP can handle the caste tensions it has been stoking. Cow-protection measures and vigilantism have hurt the cattle and leather industries, where the poor and Dalits are employed. News of the numerous incidents of harassment of Dalits by upper castes now spreads through social media. Mass Dalit anger erupted in April 2018 when tens of thousands came out on the streets in northern and western India, responding initially to a call by a relatively unknown Dalit group which dramatically snowballed on social media. The trigger was the March 2018 Supreme Court ruling on the Prevention of Atrocities Act, which is supposed to protect Dalits and Tribals from attack. In the name of 'deterring misuse', the Court made it more difficult to charge and arrest those accused. The protests intensified after nine protesters were killed in BJP-ruled states, finally forcing the BJP to bring in a bill to overturn the ruling. So far the Sangh has had considerable success in dividing Dalits, who have their own sub-caste resentments, and has assiduously sought to woo them, not least by appropriating Ambedkar as a major Indian icon. It is a reminder that a key battlefront against the Sangh remains the caste question. In the crucial state of Uttar Pradesh, the new Chief Minister, Yogi Adityanath has been appointing members of his own caste, the Thakurs (a non-Brahmin upper caste) to senior positions in the police and administration, and the Thakur community is aggressively using its muscles against other castes, both above and below.

In March 2018 the two biggest opposition parties in Uttar Pradesh–the SP, backed by the major OBC caste of Yadavs, and the BSP, backed by the majority Dalit caste of Jatavs–united to contest two state assembly seats and won both, to the dismay of the BJP, which had considered the seats impregnable.[47] In May 2018 assembly elections in the southern state of Karnataka the Congress managed to stitch up a governing coalition with the regional force, the Janata Dal (Secular) even though the BJP had emerged as the single largest party. Indeed the BJP achieved its highest ever vote share in Karnataka, testimony to how widely acceptable its ideology has become and to the inroads it has been making into the Indian South. In December 2018, the assembly election victories of the Congress in Madhya Pradesh, Rajasthan and Chhattisgarh, in each case displacing the BJP, did ring alarm bells promising a stiffer challenge in the forthcoming 2019 Lok Sabha polls. As the subsequent results therein showed, this did not materialise. As for the larger issue of making a serious challenge to Sangh hegemony is concerned, Hindutva was never put on trial anywhere in the five plus years of Modi rule. Even in Karnataka, after the May 2019 elections, the BJP through defections from the Congress and the JD(S) established its rule in Karnataka.

In the campaigning for the 2019 general elections, the BJP avoided references to the economy, making its central planks unity and national security supposedly threatened from without by Pakistan and Muslim migrations from neighbouring states, and from within by Muslim (and secularist) hostility to, and distance from, the culturally Hindu foundations of Indian nationalism. Such dangers then could only be warded off by the stewardship of 'our' Hindu strongman, Narendra Modi. The Congress focused on the deteriorating state of the economy promising special policy measures for the poor but not daring to confront the BJP on its chosen ground for fear of being branded as 'Muslim appeasers' while sharing (as did other opposition parties) the BJP's projection of a more belligerent and militaristic nationalism. On February 14, 2019 a suicide bomb attack by a local Kashmiri youth, Adil Ahmad Dar, killed 40 and injured others of the Central Reserve Police Force travelling in a bus to Srinagar. The Jaish-e-Mohammed immediately claimed responsibility releasing pictures of Dar who had joined the group earlier. Later that very month the Modi government said it had launched a successful air strike deep in Pakistan territory at Balakot where a training camp of Jaish-e-Mohammed was said to be situated. The Pakistan government responded saying Indian planes had not reached their declared target and had beaten a hasty withdrawal. Whatever the truth of the story Pulwama and what followed dramatically reinforced the BJP's main pitch for the May elections and certainly helped them electorally. In the wake of these developments the Congress and other opposition parties were all put on the defensive deciding to applaud the government for its armed response to Pulwama. Lost amidst this nationalist hubris was the fact that once again a Kashmiri had made the ultimate sacrifice to highlight the continuing opposition and resistance against Indian military occupation of the Valley.

As for the BJP's hard stand of promising to expel or otherwise punish Bangladeshi Muslims who came into Assam province during and after the upheaval caused by the 1970-71 war and had long settled there, the Congress again had no counter-narrative or proposals. It was the Congress government which had brokered an Accord in 1985 whereby non-Indian citizens would be made stateless, if not deported. The National Register of Citizens (NRC) which was to be updated to identify foreigners in Assam was only seriously put into operation under the first Modi government. In mid-2018 it produced a draft list that excluded over 4 million of Assam's total population of 33 million; while the final list in end August 2019 has excluded 1.9 million. This excludes many Bengali migrants because the reality is that vast numbers of Indians have never possessed birth certificates, passports or formalized citizenship papers. The longer-term aim of the BJP is revealed by its Citizenship Amendment Bill–which, like the situation in Assam, featured in its election campaign. This Bill would allow *only non-Muslim migrants* who came from Pakistan, Bangladesh and Afghanistan between March 24 1971 (when Bangladesh emerged) and December 31, 2014 to become in due course naturalised Indian citizens. Now that the BJP has a majority in both houses of Parliament, it was only a matter of time before this Bill would become an Act, (December 11, 2019) thereby reinforcing the idea and construction of a 'Hindu India'.

In 2014 the BJP's single majority tally was 282 out of 543 Lok Sabha seats. In 2019, it secured 303 seats with its NDA allies accounting for another 50 seats. The BJP maintained its hold on the Hindi heartland states, in the West (Gujarat and Maharashtra) and in its one southern bastion, Karnataka, while expanding for the first time into the Eastern region in Orissa and. most importantly, West Bengal. Here, it was a close second (18 seats) to the ruling Trinamool Congress (22) with the mainstream Left parties completely wiped out, getting no seats, while the Congress got two. Only the south remains relatively unconquered. The BJP/Sangh has now reached new heights of popularity and power. As we have seen, the hegemony of the BJP represents a qualitative hardening of Indian political culture. A decisive defeat for this powerful far-right bloc, so deeply engrained in the pores of Indian civil society, will require a major shift in the socio-political relationship of forces.

Notes

1. RSS: Rashtriya Swayamsevak Sangh [National Volunteer Organization], founded 1925. The first electoral party created by the RSS was the Bharatiya Jana Sangh (1951-77), which dissolved

itself into the pan-opposition Janata Party in 1977, then re-formed as the BJP in 1980.

2. Founded by an Englishman in 1885, as a forum and training ground for an all-India native political elite, the Indian National Congress was transformed by Gandhi and his colleagues after 1919 into a mass political instrument for home rule, later for independence.
3. Any claim to being (however loosely) a 'unified faith'—to carry credibility—cannot overlook the ballasts provided by the caste system. In which case Hinduism's claims to being accommodative and tolerant in any meaningfully modern sense, is absurd.
4. In 1940, the population of British and Princely State India comprised some 206m caste Hindus, 95m Muslims, 49m Scheduled Castes, 25m Tribals and 5m Sikhs.
5. See G. Balachandran, 'Religion and Nationalism in Modern India' in Kaushik Basu and Sanjay Subramanyam, eds, *Unravelling the Nation: Sectarian Conflict and India's Secular Identity*, New Delhi, 1996, pp. 108–111.
6. The unity in diversity principle itself rested on accepting one religiously constituted majority community and then other religious minorities thus shaping the nature of mass appeals which rarely sought to cut across the Hindu-Muslim/majority-minority framework. Since the commitment to 'unity' was shared in both cases this would help generate a divisive sentiment among the majority community of Hindus against Partition (and for many, against Muslims) irrespective of their loyalties to or outside the Congress. Even after independence this commitment to a unity, understood above all as territorial, meant that brutal repression of strivings for self-determination in Kashmir and in the northeast would be widely seen as a necessity deserving public support. This is a Congress legacy the BJP/Sangh is happy to emulate.
7. But the formal advocacy of this secularism by the Congress government had two consequences. It implicitly promoted Hinduism as the basic glue marking Indian society. It did allow in the name of secularism for a wider range of public dissension and criticism of the state and society and also for relatively freer

criticism of some forms of religious thinking and practices including of Brahminism and caste.

8. In 1957, Congress won 75 per cent of Lok Sabha seats with 48 per cent of the vote; in 1962, 73 per cent of seats with 45 per cent of votes; in 1967, 54 per cent of seats with 41 per cent of votes; in 1971, 67 per cent of seats with 43 per cent of votes.
9. As pointed out in the previous chapter, the new Act unlike anywhere else deliberately *criminalised* this action with up to 3 years of imprisonment for the culpable male, although marriage is a civil contract.
10. In 1952, the CPI was second in the Lok Sabha with 16 seats; in 1957 it got 27 seats; in 1962, 29 seats.
11. In 1946 the CPI mobilized a people's army and militia covering some 3,000 villages, with a population of around 3 million and took over a million acres for distribution to the landless. When New Delhi moved in, the CPI was divided on whether to continue the armed uprising or curtail it, since it shared the view that Hyderabad should be part of the Indian Union. When a section of the CPI continued the peasant struggle, the Congress government turned against and helped crush it, restoring the land to its old owners, while the Nizam himself was given the ceremonial status of a Chief Protector (*Raj Pramukh*) of the new Hyderabad state. The CPI called off the struggle in 1951 but did well in the subsequent elections.
12. It is possible that the strongly religious character of Indian society also creates the ground for highly personalized populisms to take root. This would seem evident from the popularity at times that others after Nehru down to Modi have enjoyed. But the longest lasting of hegemonies must transcend such reliance on one charismatic leader. Even if Nehru had lived longer–he died in 1964, aged 74–it is doubtful that his personal appeal could have stemmed the slide in Congress popularity, given the party's ideological and organizational limitations.
13. Ramachandra Guha, *India After Gandhi*, London, 2007, p. 137.
14. Ever since both Pakistan and India have treated the issue as a bilateral one excluding the possibility of those in the occupied

territories on both sides of the border, determining their own political future.

15. The 1949 Sunderlal Committee Report was only released in 2013 after a petition by a Cambridge student, Sunil Purushotham. See Abhirup Dam, '27,000 Massacred, Bloody Price of 'Liberation': Hyderabad 1948', September 17, 2015: www.thequint.com.
16. Pranay Gupte, *Vengeance! India After the Assassination of Indira Gandhi*, New York, 1985; pp. 195–196. Mrs. Gandhi's assassins were Sikhs.
17. See Omar Khalidi, *Khaki and Ethnic Violence in India*, New Delhi, 2003, pp. 34–35.
18. According to a former Deputy Inspector General of Police, 'No riot can continue beyond 24 hours unless the state wants it to': K.S. Subramanian, *Political Violence and the Police in India*, New Delhi, 2007, p. 80.
19. The commissions of inquiry themselves, mostly set up under Congress rule, can become a substitute for the absence of direct investigation, detection and punishment of uniformed culprits: Upendra Baxi, *Inhuman Wrongs and Human Rights: Unconventional Essays*, New Delhi, 1994.
20. Subramanian, *Political Violence and the Police in India*, pp. 49–50.
21. The cow-belt region was also the cradle of the RSS, which had a well-entrenched network of branches, cadres and affiliates there as early as 1947.
22. By comparison, Congress in 1989 won 197 seats with 40 per cent of the vote, and in 1991 won 244 seats with 36 per cent of the vote–in 2014 its nationally dispersed electorate could not compensate for its much weaker performance in the big states.
23. See Ravinder Kaur, 'The "Emerging" Middle Class', *Economic and Political Weekly*, June 28, 2014. Kaur describes these layers as aspirants to the middle class, respectful of religious leaders, consumers of well-packaged religiosity and religious-philosophical wisdoms, appreciative of Modi's strongman appeal and irritated by 'secular' talk, which is seen as ignoring their concerns while appeasing Muslims.

24. For the most comprehensive such account see Prashant Jha, *How the BJP Wins: Inside India's Greatest Election Machine*, New Delhi, 2017.
25. The result is the further 'syndicalization' of Hinduism. See Thomas Blom Hansen, 'The Vernacularisation of Hindutva', *Contributions to Indian Sociology*, Vol. 30, No. 2, 1996.
26. Badri Narayan, "The Makeover of the RSS", *The Hindu*, December 22, 2016. The RSS affiliate Bajrang Dal ['protection squad'] set up in 1984 comprises lumpen/unemployed youth who attack marked-out targets, absolving other Sangh affiliates from responsibility for violence.
27. Vikas Pathak, 'RSS reports sharp rise in shakas in 2018', *The Hindu*, March 10, 2018. In 1948 the RSS had 600,000 members, In 1970 The RSS became the largest voluntary organisation in the country. RSS *shakas* rose from around 10,000 in 1977 to 30,238 in 1994. See C. Jaffrelot, *The Hindu Nationalist Movement and Indian Politics*, Penguin, New Delhi 1999, pp. 75, 238, 529.
28. It is an unwritten rule in India that neither the mainstream media nor the leaders of opposition parties will delve into or make public the personal sex lives and foibles of their opponents. That dimension will have to await a future biographer of Modi.
29. Fourteen years younger than Modi, the heavy-jowled Gujarati was a youthful recruit to the RSS in Ahmedabad and has been by his side since the 1980s, holding twelve portfolios in the Gujarat state government when Modi was chief minister there. Trailed by allegations of dirty dealing, including murder, Shah has been a key electoral strategist for Modi and claims to have driven up BJP membership to around 180 million, exceeding that of the Chinese Communist Party. Although one can become a party member simply by registering through a mobile 'missed call' this still says a lot about the party's general public appeal.
30. India's richest man and owner of the biggest corporation, Reliance Industries Limited, Mukesh Ambani, is also the top media moghul after acquiring Network 18 TV group, part of the Eenadu group of newspapers in the South and starting the 4G mobile network, Jio. For a detailed survey see, Paranjoy Guha Thakurta,

'Future of Alternative Media', in Ashish Kothari and K.J. Joy, eds., *Alternative Futures: India Unshackled*, Authors Upfront, New Delhi, 2017. Guha Thakurta is a former Editor of the *Economic and Political Weekly*.

31. Times News Network, 'Amit Shah most followed Indian politician after PM on Twitter', *Times of India*, March 7, 2018. By September 2016 over 367 million Indians had internet connectivity. See Aarati Krishnan, 'How many Indians have Internet?' *The Hindu*, March 26, 2017.
32. Swati Chaturvedi, *I am a Troll: Inside the secret world of the BJP's digital army*, New Delhi 2016.
33. See the *Frontline* special issue, 'Higher Education in Peril', August 2018.
34. Though successive Congress governments from Nehru's time onwards had substantially whittled down the original powers given to J&K, Article 370 could only be overturned by the J&K Constituent Assembly which dissolved itself in November 1956 and has never been reconstituted since.
35. See 'Assam Up in Arms as Army Chief Wades into Political Territory', *The Wire*, February 28, 2018; 'Olive green former Army Chief Gen. V.K. Singh dons RSS Uniform', *National Herald*, 2 March 2018. Singh is currently Minister of State for Road and Transport. During the first BJP-led government under Vajpayee, ex-servicemen, including retired generals, were systematically recruited into party politics. This had never happened on such a scale before. In private settings the officer corps now gives free voice to anti-Muslim prejudices.
36. According to the Report "India: Vigilante 'Cow Protection' Groups Attack Minorities" released on February 18, 2019 by Human Rights Watch, between May 2015 and December 2018, 44 people–36 Muslims–were killed across 12 states while 280 were injured across 20 states. Hate crime watch, a database of the Indian organisation FactChecker reported 254 incidents of crimes targeting religious minorities between January 2009 and October 2018 in which 91 were killed and 579 injured. Around 90 per cent of these attacks occurred after the BJP came to power

in May 2014 with 66 per cent taking place in BJP-ruled states. Of the victims 62 per cent were Muslims and 14 per cent Christians. These were attacks on inter-faith couples, communal clashes and cow and religious conversion related acts of violence. See https://hrw.org/2019/02/18/violent-cow-protection-india/vigilante-groups-attack-minorities

37. To take some examples: a former DIG of Police in Gujarat, D.G. Vanzara charged in 2007 for conducting fake 'encounter killings'—when police shoot on sight, allegedly in self-defence—was released on bail in 2015, with charges dismissed in 2017. Charges against Amit Shah for involvement in the same killing were dropped when the BJP won the 2014 election. Charges against the Sangh's female preacher, Sadhvi Pragya Thakur, related to a 2006 bomb-blast in the Muslim-majority town of Malegaon were dropped by the NIA in 2016, while her alleged co-conspirator, Lt Col. S.K. Purohit was bailed out in 2017. In April 2018 the NIA acquitted all five accused of a 2007 bombing at a famous mosque in Hyderabad, which killed 9 and injured 58 Muslims during Friday prayers. Rohini Sailan, a special prosecutor in this case (since retired) publicly stated that she had been pressured to 'go slow' on the accused.
38. "Ruling BJP bags 95% of funds" at www.adrindia.org
39. In March 2018 Congress MPs circulated an impeachment motion calling for an inquiry into Misra's 'misbehaviour'. This was dismissed by the Head of the Rajya Sabha, despite ample *prima facie* evidence of wrongdoing, and Congress subsequently withdrew the motion. See Aditya A. K.'s litigation news report on the *Bar & Bench* website March 29, 2018.
40. Tactically, it was Indira Gandhi's 1975–77 period of emergency rule that gave the Jan Sangh, precursor to the BJP, its springboard into national office when it joined the post-Emergency umbrella coalition of opposition parties under Morarji Desai.
41. Atul Kohli, 'Politics of Economic Growth in India, 1980–2005, Part 1', *Economic and Political Weekly*, April 8, 2006.
42. In *The Painful Transition* (1990) I borrowed Stuart Hall's term 'authoritarian democracy' to describe the dynamics of the Indian

polity in the 1980s and the risk that the balance between the two components was shifting for the worse.

43. V.P. Singh was a former Congress minister expelled by Rajiv Gandhi for uncovering the immensely corrupt relations between the Congress leadership and international arms manufacturers—the Bofors Scandal. He led a coalition of smaller opposition parties, the National Front, which governed with the external, conditional support of the Left and the BJP from 1989 to 1991.
44. See 'Syndicated Hinduism' in Romila Thapar, *The Historian and Her Craft: Collected Essays and Lectures*, Vol. 4, New Delhi 2017.
45. In fact, the BJP vote only fell from 24 to 22 per cent between 1999 and 2004, while its seat tally fell from 182 to 138. The Congress share of the vote actually dropped from 28 to 27 per cent, while its seat tally rose from 114 to 145, thanks to the distortions of the first-past-the-post constituency system.
46. Total employment dropped by 0.4 per cent, from 480.4 million to 467.6m, between 2013-14 and 2015-16. See Vinoj Abrahm, 'Stagnant Employment Growth' in *Economic and Political Weekly*, September 23, 2017; Radhicka Kapoor, 'A job crisis, in figures', *Indian Express*, December 13, 2017. The 'employment elasticity of output' figure which averaged 0.4 between 1983 and 1993/4 fell to 0.01 in the last decade. Malini Goyal, 'What needs to be done—and is being done—to employ more Indians, and to make them employable', *Economic Times*, May 21, 2017.
47. SP: Samajwadi Party (Socialist Party); BSP: Bahujan Samaj Party (Downtrodden Party).

4

Modi's Second Term: Hindutva Marching Ahead

A Tectonic Shift

A far-right authoritarian populism, establishing mass identification with a 'Supreme Leader' as the embodiment of the 'popular will', has triumphed. There are unmistakable similarities here with the carefully constructed appeal and style of fascist-type formations. On one hand, there has been this shift towards greater personalisation of politics. Over time this shift towards greater personalisation has been promoted by the policy convergences of the main contenders for power while the technological transformations in the forms and patterns of mass communication have made the skills of image projection increasingly influential for a public whose attention span or interest in rational debate and argument has diminished. On the other hand, there is the huge support base of the BJP and even more importantly the millions of members and the more active cadres belonging to one or the other of the organisations of the Sangh Parivar. These cadres screwed down the ideological moorings of Hindu nationalism with its Modi exemplar where it did not exist, and reinforced those moorings where it already existed.

In the arena of competing Indian nationalisms, Hindu nationalism has expanded its geographical reach and raised its emotional intensity. At one time it could have been said that relative to the total Hindu population only a 'fringe', mobilised by Hindutva, forces, truly hated Muslims while a much larger section of Hindus was indifferent to the plight of Muslims who along with Dalits and Adivasis, belong to the most deprived sections of society. But, as these elections show, a much stronger spectrum of emotions vis-a-vis Muslims, from fear to contempt to anger to hatred, now prevails among much wider sections of Hindus: witness the comfortable victory of the hate-filled Sadhvi, Pragya Singh Thakur. Modi himself made viciously communal statements during his campaigning (other BJP candidates were as bad or worse) which, according to existing rules, should have led to his punishment by the Election Commission (EC). The EC, by a majority of two to one, refused to take any such steps indicating how suborned this institution, among others, has already become to the ruling establishment. Is it a coincidence that in August 2019 the Income Tax department, in the name of tax evasion, began probes into the business and professional activities of the wife, sister and son of Ashok Lavasa, the now retired member of the Election Commission who had specifically named Modi and Amit Shah as violating the rules banning communal statements and appeals during the 2019 election campaign?[1]

What Now?

The Congress prioritised its own electoral revival above alliances with other regional parties, especially in the Hindi heartland. This meant maximising the number of its own candidates. It refused to make concessions to the BSP or SP in the states where it was strong like Madhya Pradesh and Rajasthan, as part of an overall deal. This strategy comprehensively failed. Despite its status as the second party it is now, like the other opposition parties, essentially a regional force. Those other parties have no national, let alone international, vision or programme, but are simply locked into the limited horizons of wanting to strengthen and expand beyond their existing sectoral and regional bases. The Congress Party to revamp itself is talking of possible leadership changes away from the dynasty. But this is to dodge its problem–of establishing a distinctive ideology and vision, something it cannot achieve. Nationally, the Congress will not move away from a soft Hindutva, indeed more voices within the party are demanding a more open courting of Hindu majoritarianism. Nor will it abandon economic neoliberalism but may only argue for a more compensatory version. Internationally, the Congress wants to build a 'strong India' on much the same lines of the BJP. In the coming years the party, far from seeing rejuvenation, is more likely to split or break-up, although this cannot be deemed certain. As it is, many senior party members, including MLAs who were once in the Congress camp began defecting to the BJP. Goa and Karnataka were recent instances of this trend.

For the new BJP administration the transformation of the domestic arena is again its paramount concern. Regarding the economy, the BJP will do everything to remain the preferred party of Indian capital and this includes a more systematic assault on organised labour. The draft papers on four new labour codes prepared in Modi's first term can now, with minor concessions, depending on the strength of resistance, be pushed into law. As earlier, selective welfare sops for a deeply atomised labour force may well feature. Similarly, in foreign policy there will be more of the same: consolidating the strategic relationship with the US against China plus two BJP flourishes–deeper connections between India and Israel, certainly as already shown, more muscle-flexing and bravado vis-à-vis Pakistan.

One can be sure that the political executive, headed by the Prime Minister and his Office, will now go all out to control and suborn all government agencies including those having by law substantial autonomy of operation from the executive such as the repressive apparatuses, the top investigating agencies, central and state educational bodies, the civil services, the top economic and financial watchdog bodies like the Reserve Bank of India. Furthermore, the creation and consolidation of a Hindu India and state, in which other religious minorities not deemed to fall under the Hindu umbrella, are to be relegated to second class citizenship status, must involve major changes in laws below the level of the Constitution.

The end goal here is not the establishment of a one-party dictatorship headed by a 'Supremo' but of a fundamentally undemocratic order that retains some democratic features. The majority Hindu population will certainly enjoy special individual and group rights denied to other religious minorities. The model is in many respects that of Israel, an anti-democratic because a Jewish state, which since it has certain democratic features including regular elections can, in the eyes of far too many, falsely pass itself off as a genuine democracy, albeit with some unfortunate undemocratic aspects. With the National Democratic Alliance (NDA) having close to a two-thirds majority in the lower house and well on its way to securing an expanding majority in the upper house over the next five years, there will be efforts to bring in constitutional amendments of the kind that the BJP/Sangh have always wanted. With the help of allies in the Rajya Sabha, the BJP secured the Constitutional Amendment Act (CAA)–the necessary prelude to carrying out a National Population Register (NPR) in 2020 to secure the household and personal data base after which the National Register of Citizens (NRC) will adjudicate on who are 'doubtful citizens' or 'non-citizens' to be deprived of basic rights and even put in detention camps.

The BJP's policy tracks can be put under four basic themes: (1) Expanding its political presence and dominance by suborning and eliminating electoral competitors. (2) Keeping Christians and Muslims "in their place" and particular attention to be paid to the latter by terrorising, ghettoising and inferiorising them i.e. reducing them de facto (and to the extent possible *de jure*) to second class citizenship status. (3) Ideological homogenisation. (4) Not the completely elimination but the hollowing out of the structures of democracy and federalism.

1. The BJP secured enormous funding from corporate donors and foreign supporters for its election campaigns in 2019 and is by far the richest of all the parties. Using this money power the BJP will seek to buy off MLAs and MPs of other

parties and depose opposition-controlled state governments, Congress and others. This strategy has already proved successful in Karnataka. Elections held in October 2019 in Haryana and Maharashtra saw the BJP emerge as the senior partner in a two party coalition government with a new formation, the JJP (Jannayak Janta Party or Public Servants People's Party) in the first case. In Maharashtra compared to the ruling alliance earlier and now, the BJP lost ground in terms of seats to its partner, the Shiv Sena. But there was only a marginal loss in the BJP's vote share. But the pre-poll alliance of the two parties broke down after the elections with Uddhav Thackeray, leader of the Shiv Sena claiming that the BJP in announcing that its regional leader Devendra Fadnavis would lead the Maharashtra government for the next five years, betrayed its earlier promise to rotate the Chief Ministership between the two parties. Thackeray thus forged a separate majority-winning alliance with the Nationalist Congress Party (NCP) and the Congress Party to install himself as the new Chief Minister in a government comprising rival forces and different ideologies–the Shiv Sena after all, is explicitly pro-Hindutva. It remains to be seen whether this alliance will hold together at all, and if so, for how long? In Haryana the BJP lost its earlier seat majority on its own and has had to settle for a new governing alliance but it actually got a higher vote share than in the previous state assembly elections.

2. (i) Under the new CAA (including its Statement of Objectives and Reasons) non-Muslim minorities from Bangladesh, Pakistan and Afghanistan are deemed to be religiously persecuted and can get fast-track naturalization and permanent residence in India. Regarding citizenship the SC has in an earlier verdict shifted the onus of proof away from the government and on to the accused. In effect, like Israel's right of return for all Jews, the aim is to initiate (perhaps as a starter) at least some kind of a neighbourhood 'right of return' for Hindus in South Asia. Then, as a result

of these twin proposed measures, Muslims who don't have officially prescribed documentation to prove their citizenship status can be detained, expelled or deprived of certain basic citizenship rights; and even their progeny born in India will be permanently denied citizenship. Non-Muslims caught in the same web will not suffer such treatment and can apply for fast-track naturalization.

The CAA-NPR-NRC combined project has two main purposes. One is to punish Muslims primarily but also to put many others who are poor, dependent on the 'good will' of this government for their daily survival, i.e. taming and controlling those whose hardships might make them more rebellious. The second purpose is to collect massive data to create a stronger surveillance state for all Indians. What the BJP/Sangh did not expect is the popular sustained upsurge–not initiated or dominated by opposition parties–but by students and youth across religious faiths and by ordinary Muslims on a huge scale. Both have united for the first time, along with many other liberals, leftists and once apolitical citizens, all of whom rightly recognize that this project is aimed at undermining Indian secularism and therefore its democracy as well as trying to polarize ordinary Hindus against Muslims. That students and youth organizations (except for the ABVP) are resisting is an expression of the pent-up anger at brutal assaults by police in universities against democratic student activism on various fronts since 2014. Can this official project be derailed?

Continued and growing mass resistance can push the SC to rule against the CAA which is unconstitutional. This mass struggle can also, if it grows, push the non-BJP states to not carry out the NPR. Two states–Kerala and West Bengal have done so–more must join. This can force the BJP to back down or else go in for an emergency-like situation which is not what it wants. Regardless of the final outcome, a strong ray of hope has emerged and there will be more recruits for the longer struggle against Hindutva. The deliberate assault on JNU by masked intruders enjoying apparent police complicity has added more fuel to the fire.

(ii) As part of the process of pushing for the further ghettoisation and terrorisation of Muslims, routinised micro-level violence against Muslims by Hindutva acolytes very much serves as a stimulus to this end. Such vigilante attacks will essentially go unpunished by the law-and-order machinery subservient to local political authorities in BJP-ruled states. For Muslims matters are clear. Accept the new India. Keep your heads down in your ghettos. Functional interactions and work exchanges are fine but greatly limit socially intermingling with Hindus. Don't publicise your faith let alone seek to convert others. [In the coming period the BJP may well want to put forward an all-India anti-conversion bill excluding Hindu "re-conversions", of course.]. Don't politically resist the BJP or Sangh by joining or supporting other parties, and show more obedience by politically and electorally supporting the BJP. In return, they will be left to live in relative peace on the terms set by the ruling dispensation and its supporters. These implicit injunctions are in fact being followed by many Muslims in Gujarat, providing the BJP with a desired template for other states.

But what may be desired is not necessarily going to be what happens. What has now been done in J&K will have a polarising effect on Muslims in the rest of India who otherwise never felt strongly about the Kashmir issue which was distant from their everyday concerns. This will correctly be seen as having a wider political purpose–the subordination and humiliation of Muslims everywhere in the country–because this was as much an attack on the dignity and self-respect of their being Muslims as on their being Kashmiris. Should this lead to repeated eruptions of armed action by some Muslim individuals and groups then this will create a dynamic of deepening communal polarisation. This means the Gujarat formula for peace through Muslims quietly accepting their subordination throughout the country may well turn out to be an illusion. For one thing the agitation against CAA/NRC is testimony to Muslims throughout the country increasingly seeing themselves as a beseiged community whose very existence as Indian citizens is now under great threat. Not since 1947 or even before have we seen such a collective mass resistance by this community as to this government.

3. To bring about much greater ideological homogenisation, the key is to have greater and lasting control of (a) educational institutions, public or private, and (b) the media. The first can be pursued through curriculum changes, regulation from above, appointment of loyalists and sympathisers to teaching positions, harassment of private institutions unwilling to cooperate. Regarding the print and electronic media, one can use money power and government pressures to suborn them. Controlling social media may not be possible in the same way, but what can and is being done is to ensure that Hindutva narratives are maximised through troll armies and closer relations with digital giants like Facebook, Google and WhatsApp which, as basically business enterprises, will see the value of cooperating with governments in various ways, including through prioritising their messaging. By giving Bollywood the formal status of an 'industry', the government is now freer to intervene through penalties and financial carrots to better control film content and distribution. This is not to speak of closer and stronger exercise of censorship rules which is already evident.

4. The BJP/Sangh will monitor and subdue actual or potential dissenters among civil society actors and groups, including recalcitrant NGOs, popular movements protesting government policies or against Hindutva beliefs and practices. Stronger and newer mechanisms of surveillance will be put in place. Here, making the wider use of Aadhar obligatory will help. Nor should we forget that quite apart from periodic physical assaults by groups against even non-Muslims whom they perceive to be their opponents, there is also the widespread resort to greater censorship of speech through accusations of being "anti-national". This is carried out by various formal authority structures while at another level there is now much more widespread filing by individuals and groups close to the Sangh, of police FIRs and defamation suits on such grounds. This then leads to at least prolonged legal and financial harassment of those accused. Here the process itself is the punishment.

Existing anti-democratic and repressive laws, such as those on sedition, impunity for armed forces no matter their crimes, preventive detention on the mere grounds of suspicion of terrorism or of possibly carrying out unlawful acts–must all be retained and even extended. The Unlawful Activities Prevention Act (UAPA) has recently been amended to drastically widen the ambit of terrorism by allowing the designation of individuals as terrorists. This can be any individual who is said to be guilty of helping to "prepare" for a terrorist act or to "promote" terrorism. Leave aside the difficulty in achieving a consensus over the definition of terrorism itself, the terms "prepare" and "promote" are deliberately left so vague in their meaning that there is effectively a *carte blanche* for the law enforcing agencies to deem whomever they see fit as a terrorist.

Let us also not forget the efforts of the BJP to make government functioning more opaque. From above, the government has sought to influence, if not control, the Central Information Commission (CIC) which was set up as an independent body under the Right to Information (RTI) Act of 2005 to oversee and ensure greater transparency, responsiveness and obedience to the Act's rules regarding the duties and responsibilities of government servants facing public requests for information about institutional functioning and decisions. This has been done through the government now giving itself the right to decide the length of tenure and the salaries of the Chief and other senior members of the CIC. From below, there have been actual physical assaults and killings of RTI activists who very often are seen as leaders pursuing justice in their local communities.[2]

Much has already been said in the previous essay on "Two Hegemonies" about the Sangh's suborning of democratic institutions. The shameful SC ruling on Ayodhya was mentioned there.[3] Here it must be stressed that this verdict makes clear how minimal resistance will be posed to the course pursued by Hindutva. The judiciary supposedly the one body meant to be independent enough to check the power of the executive in the name of secularism, democracy and justice has shown that it will provide little resistance. Making matters worse is that all the opposition parties including the mainstream left either welcomed the decision or, even while making criticisms, called for the public acceptance of the ruling not daring to condemn unequivocally the verdict or the role of the SC.

If it is important to understand the future implications of that verdict there is also the need to explore in some detail what the fall-out will be of the fact that Kashmir's autonomy has been negated and the manner in which this was done. This has serious implications for Indian democracy in general and for its federalism in particular. But the historically distinctive pattern of J&K's incorporation into the Union, the never fully submerged desire of many in the Valley for independence, the sovereign claims over the region by two bitter neighbourhood rivals each now nuclearly armed, all give the Kashmir question on its own an exceptional gravitas. What the future holds in this respect is deeply worrying.

Ending Kashmir's Autonomy

The annulment of Article 370 fulfilled the longstanding and publicly declared aim of the forces of Hindu Nationalism that

J&K, as the only Muslim majority state in the Indian Union, must not be allowed to exist. Along with the legal annulments, New Delhi not only bifurcated the region into two parts–Jammu and Kashmir on one hand, and Ladakh on the other–but for the first time in the history of Indian federalism, downgraded the status of the region from statehood making the two parts mere "Union Territories" and therefore much more subordinated to central rule. Of the seven such UTs that already exist in the Indian Union, two have been allowed to have a representative legislative; J&K will join them, while Ladakh will join the others without such a legislative body.

This action was long prepared. In Modi's last term before the 2019 general elections, "President's Rule" had been imposed to deny any possibility of a state government being formed by the main local parties with a strong base particularly in the Kashmir Valley, precisely to prepare the ground for the August 5 Presidential order of annulment. In the days before that announcement Modi's government sent an additional 38,000 troops (much more, according to some private observers) to join the existing force of over 750,000 armed personnel in the Kashmir Valley, worsening the already worst ratio in the world of armed personnel to civilians, standing at 1 to around 10. This was to ensure the comprehensive and utterly undemocratic lockdown so as to prevent any public display of opposition. The BJP/Sangh motivation is not just a reassertion of the principle of prioritizing territorial unity; it is also motivated by a foundational hatred of Muslims and Islam and determination to reduce Indian Muslims to second-class citizens as part of its drive to establish a Hindu nation and state in all but name. This action has consequences specifically for the three parts of the region, for the rest of India, and for India's relations with Pakistan.

The abrogation was carried out through a brazen violation of the Constitution. The fundamental basis on which the region was incorporated into the Union was through the sovereign authority of a J&K Constituent Assembly set up in 1951 and permanently dissolved in 1956. While a state legislature–which can never have sovereign authority but only a representative authority–was repeatedly used to make modifications and shift more and more powers embodied in the Indian Constitution to the province, the annulment of Article 370 can only be done by that Constituent Assembly. To get around this, the Modi government used another Article 367 to introduce a clause to make a state legislature the equivalent of a constituent assembly. Then if a state assembly is not in operation because, for example, President's Rule has been imposed, this allows the President to usurp the powers of this assembly and issue ordinances that become law. Given this unconstitutional equation the next step was then to nullify Article 370 and following this, scrap Article 35A which prevented private land sales or state government post to those not domiciled in J&K.

Modi has said that statehood would be restored to Jammu and Kashmir in time, and polls for the new legislature would be held. This promise has been made because while removal of 35A is necessary to bring about demographic changes in Jammu and Kashmir, the local BJP party unit in Jammu is worried about outsiders taking over land. So at the right time, after some land is given over to favoured capitalists from other states, then, as in a few other Indian states, such land acquisition can then take place but only for those having domiciled certificates thus partially restoring local privileges. The real game plan however is this: A Delimitation Commission has already been set up to reorganize constituencies and administrative districts/units, and will complete its job before elections are held. One aim is to change administrative units to more easily ghettoize Muslims through concentrating them in greater numbers, so making it easier to monitor and exercise control over them in the future. The other aim is to increase the number of constituencies in Hindu-majority Jammu (with a population close to 6 million, of which around 35 per cent are Muslims), which has a bigger territory but a smaller overall population than the Valley (which has close to 8 million)–so that the BJP, which has massive support in Jammu but very little in the Valley, can nonetheless obtain an overall majority of seats on its own or with smaller parties outside the bigger Kashmiri ones.

There could also be another legal-political manoeuvre. Historically, the RSS has always wanted trifurcation and therefore separate statehood for the Jammu region as well. Once this government is confident that it can secure a majority in the new legislature for the Union Territory of Jammu and Kashmir, this could provide the legal path to a further bifurcation whereby Jammu gets statehood while Kashmir could well remain a UT with maximalist forms of political-military control, to be enduringly exercised over it by the Centre. The Modi government took the unique step of both bifurcating and then demoting both parts of a former unified state to UT status, but also ensuring that one part can have a representative legislative body but not the other. At the same time, Modi gave a reassurance–surely more directed at the Hindus of Jammu than at the Muslims who comprise 96 per cent of the people in the Valley–that he is concerned about their interests and that some of their special privileges will be restored through re-establishment of statehood.

If the annulment of Article 370 was Kashmir specific, the downgrading from statehood to UT status carries broader implications for what can happen to Indian federalism and the country as a whole. Hindutva today wants to centralize as much power and authority as possible so as to impose a stronger uniformity across India. Here the immense diversities of language, religion, topography, history, customs, the various political parties and provincial governments, as well as the regional unevenness of economic development has always, objectively speaking, stood as the biggest barrier to the Hindutva project. The periodic declarations from Sangh spokespersons about the need for "One Nation, One Poll", "One Nation, One Language", "One Nation, One Leader", One Nation, One [identity] Card" are a way of 'testing the waters' of public political discourse, of trying to normalize consideration of what were earlier considered outlandish or unacceptable ideas at odds with the need to preserve India's socio-cultural diversity and its political federalism. If the SC allows this government to get away with the manner in which it has abused existing legislative and executive powers to change the status of J&K then it will have given the Centre the Damocles Sword of 'arbitrary territorial and political re-organisation' to hang over the heads of all the states that make up the larger Union.

But to return to Kashmir: In the Valley, the 'middle ground' of those who have wanted to remain in India–albeit with much reduced autonomy but with a willingness to collaborate with the powers that be in New Delhi–have been wiped off the political map. Where can they go now? Can they join the separatists, or do they try to collaborate with a government that no longer needs them unless they are willing to become complete puppets and abandon all talk of autonomy? In the Valley, there will be growing anger and deeper and wider public alienation from the rest of India, especially among the youth. There will very likely be greater recruitment and support for, as well as collaboration with, cross-border insurgent forces–themselves abetted by the Pakistan government. This, and even non-violent mass actions, will be taken as an excuse by the Indian government and armed forces for the exercise of greater brutality and repression, including the use of the newly amended legislations on 'terrorism' to arbitrarily and pre-emptively arrest, harass, and even torture those deemed 'suspects'.

The BJP has also now decisively altered its relationship with Pakistan. It is an *enemy* with whom there can be no accommodation except on Indian terms i.e. accepting this new reality. This is the external counterpart to its Hindutva hostility towards Muslims internally. And the "anti-Pakistan" banner can rally around a much larger section of the Indian population including huge numbers of liberals, mainstream leftists, supporters and leaders of the Congress, and other non-BJP parties who otherwise oppose the BJP. The period when some kind of bilateral 'soft border' arrangement, or even some form of 'dual guardianship,' of a relatively autonomous Kashmir on both sides of the border, could be put in place is over. The message to the rest of the world is clear: Kashmir is not to appear on any international agenda. It is purely an internal matter brooking no external interference, humanitarian considerations be damned.

Some progressives in Pakistan who want to institutionalize liberal democracy in Pakistan may see a decisive erosion of the political power of the Pakistani military in Modi's moves in Kashmir. The stalemate, they could say, has ended. Both countries now have swallowed their respective parts of the once-united J&K province and will have to move towards accepting the new international *fait accompli*, since surely neither side is stupid enough to risk a major war given the nuclear overhang. But matters are not so simple. Both the Pakistan military establishment and Islamist forces in the country are not going to take this route. Indeed, Modi's India, through its earlier strike on Balakot, well into Pakistani territory–the first time since the nuclear age began that one nuclear power has carried out such a deep penetration, conventional air strike on another nuclear power–has indicated that Pakistan's so-called nuclear shield will not deter conventional assaults on it by the much stronger Indian forces. To be sure, Pakistan is aware of India's conventional superiority and has publicly drawn up its own red lines that declare its willingness to use tactical nuclear weapons on Indian troops who enter too far into its territory. India's nuclear doctrine, however, simply says it reserves the right to retaliate wherever Indian troops are threatened. The latest interpretation of its nuclear "No First Use" doctrine by a former foreign secretary official is that this does not preclude pre-emptive use if circumstances warrant it.[4] The real danger is not so much that one side will decide to launch its nuclear weapons, but that the likelihood of cross-border insurgency will grow after the US-Pakistan agreement over Afghanistan frees more Islamist squads to move towards the Indo-Pakistan border areas. Cross-border skirmishes along this border can rise significantly. These can turn into a conventional war, raising the chances of a miscalculated or inadvertent nuclear exchange breaking out. Pakistani efforts to internationalise the issue, short of a threat of nuclear exchange emerging, will not really succeed. For the United States India's weight in its geopolitical structure of alliances is greater than its ties with Pakistan, though for Washington these are separate relationships serving non-substitutable concerns. As for China, it will give some verbal support and perhaps supply arms to Pakistan but nothing more.

In the rest of India, Modi's move gained him even greater popularity among the general public with most regional parties, including some of those opposed to the BJP like Delhi's ruling AAP (Common Man's Party) hailing it. The mainstream electoral left of the CPM, CPI and an above ground Maoist party, the CPI-ML (Liberation) called for the restoration of the previous status quo, even willing to call for extending greater autonomy. The Congress Party is divided. Some leaders are calling to restore the previous status quo, while others have publicly approved the final outcome but criticised the legal means used to achieve it as well as the temporary clampdown in the Valley, but nothing else. Many legitimate fears have been expressed about the assault on Indian federalism, the momentum that is being generated for the anti-democratic means that are being and will be used in future pursuit of the Hindutva agenda. But when it comes to the question of preserving 'national security' there is no dissent: Kashmir must remain a part of India.

The Central Issue

Herein lies the basic dilemma. Everything hinges on the evolving situation in Kashmir over the coming decades and generations. For over 70 years the Kashmiri people have repeatedly expressed their desire to retain their distinct status. All want de-militarisation but have disagreed along three separate lines as to the way forward. Those political parties, namely, the National Conference (NC) with its rival the People's Democratic Party (PDP), want to remain in India and practice patronage-based clientelism, and therefore have been content with playing the games of power-brokering and deal-making with New Delhi, electoral competition, and unprincipled alliances with each other and with the local Congress Party unit in J&K. The PDP even forged a coalition government with Modi's BJP before the latter withdrew its support and imposed President's Rule. Then there are the parties and groups that espouse some form of separatism either to join Pakistan or be independent but are hardly involved in underground struggle. They are kept under much tighter central control and frequently harassed and leaders detained.

It is the underground movement that has been mainly responsible for organising non-violent mass mobilizations and engaging in retaliatory violence against the brutality of the occupation. This is primarily waged by local Kashmiris, young and old. Although there is certainly an influx of various insurgent groups from across the border, it is a myth that it is these militants (or 'terrorists,' as they are called in officialese), are the reason for such a heavy presence of the Indian armed forces. By New Delhi's own account, these 'terrorists', home grown or Pakistani, are today said to number a few hundred–much less than the couple of thousands said to have been there at the peak of militancy in the 1990s. In neither case can it be plausibly argued that you need 750,000 and more armed personnel to keep such numbers in check.

This ending of autonomy is not going to be reversed by any future Indian government. Yet given the way Kashmiris have for so long behaved vis-a-vis the longstanding Indian occupation, there is no reason to doubt that their resistance will continue and that many more will not want to be a part of the Indian Union. If an ever increasing majority in the Valley, perhaps joined by more and more Muslims in Jammu, move in this direction, what can be expected? Certainly, this will lead to an enduring and even more brutal military repression by the BJP/Sangh. Should the resistance continue and deepen, more people in Pakistan, in the wider Muslim world, and perhaps elsewhere, will begin to stir and lend more material and political support to it. But what of progressives in India who are already horrified by what the Modi government has done and what it is likely to do in the future?

If the middle ground in Kashmir has been destroyed, what of those in the rest of India who are opposed to Indian brutality in Kashmir but are not willing to respect the right of the Kashmiris to determine their own political future up to and including secession? The classic Leninist and truly democratic formula has always been that an oppressed community like the Kashmiris must have the right to decide their own political future which in this case could be (a) fighting for greater autonomy within India; (b) independence; or (c) merger with Pakistan. No prominent liberal intellectual or even any leader of the mainstream Communist parties after August 5 has publicly taken such a stand. Powerful and legitimate criticisms of what has been done abound as also sound extrapolations of the democratic dangers that are now arising from what has been done. But the territorial unity of India remains effectively 'sacred' for them.

The point, however, is that one can disagree with the manner in which Kashmiris might want to exercise that right, e.g., by wanting independence or even joining with Pakistan; and even seek to persuade them not to choose that particular path and remain to fight for a democratic India. But the rock-bottom democratic principle is *respecting their right to choose*. This means categorically opposing all efforts by the Indian government to forcibly prevent them from exercising that choice in the future. The best thing would be for separate, binding referendums to be held in Ladakh, in Jammu, and in the Valley reflecting the three choices of being with India, being with Pakistan, or independence. We know that the majority in the first two regions would choose to remain and the third to be separate. We also know that no such referendums will ever be offered. What then is the point of taking such a stand? It is simply that today and in the future, the only truly honest and courageous way to show solidarity with the suffering of the Kashmiri people is to declare this. To only oppose all forms of force that might or will be used against Kashmiris is not enough, since the main end for which that force is being used–to prevent territorial separation–is something that one silently accepts as a state of affairs that must never be allowed to happen, no matter what the principal sufferers themselves may wish to choose.

In the coming months and years, there will be many occasions on which all kinds of non-Kashmiri Indian progressives will have to come together to oppose governmental violence against Kashmiris. Our different preferences for what we consider to be the best future for Kashmiris must not prevent this practical unity in struggle. At the same time we must never be silent accomplices with the powers that would seek to deny the oppressed people of Kashmir the right not only to choose but, more importantly, to *freely* pursue their goal of collective self-determination.

A Long Term Struggle

Hindutva's broad hegemony is here to stay for the foreseeable future. Its rise has been part of a worldwide phenomenon, one of whose key underlying causes has been the material and emotional turmoil created by a globalising neoliberal economic order but expressed politically and culturally in nationally specific ways. But this is a much longer term problem and threat in India than rightwing authoritarian populisms/nationalisms in other countries for two major reasons. One, no other far-right force comes close to matching the Sangh Parivar's implantation in the pores of Indian civil society. We are talking of a party, the BJP, which now claims to be the world's largest with some 180 million members, admittedly because a mobile 'missed call' is enough to establish membership. But this still says something about how big is the constituency wanting to become at least passive members. Second, in the various countries that have witnessed the rise of right wing and far-right populisms whether from above or below, such as The Philippines, Brazil, France, Hungary, Poland, etc., there are other political parties (conservative, right wing and those claiming to be centre-left) of some significant strength which separately or through electoral alliances can hope or expect to achieve state power or, over time, displace the far-right from that pedestal. In India one-party rule is hegemonic also because the whole of the opposition is so fragmented and weak in comparison that even if they come together they don't match up. The issue is not that the BJP's electoral dominance is permanent or incontestable. Future electoral reversals in response to the BJP's governing failures or in reaction to acute crisis situations, economic or otherwise, can propel even a rag tag bunch of smaller parties, including the Congress (assuming it is around), to collective prominence even at the centre. But this will not decisively erode the hegemony of Hindutva, let alone destroy it for good.

Destroying Hindutva is the central task and there is no option but to recognise that this more fundamental struggle is going to be very long. One development could suddenly foreshorten this time scale. That would be the emergence of a dramatic political shift to the left in one of the advanced capitalist countries, such as in UK or the US, because the much more interconnected character of the world means political and social, and not just economic, shock waves in one part of the world travel faster than ever to other parts. But barring such unforeseeable and unpredictable events, what are the ways to go about this struggle in India? I will assess five possible pathways which do cross and connect with each other at times but have their own distinctive directions and ultimate goals.

A. Work to revamp and rejuvenate the existing parties in opposition. Here, there is no getting away from the Congress Party. Among liberals, one side says the Congress should fade away by merging into a newer coalition or body that is more coherent, and not a stitching up of parties with different interests, programmes and aims. The other side insists that for all its limitations, the Congress is still the tallest among the opposition forces, has repeatedly ruled at the Centre, and remains, no matter how tarnished, the principal legatee of the secular and democratic values created by the National Movement and the Constitution.

   Either way, this is a disastrous strategy and not only because the Congress (and all other bourgeois regional parties) remain beholden to capital and support, in one way or the other, the neoliberal project. At best the eventual construction of a still right wing but somewhat less communal and more liberal political-electoral counterweight (whether the Congress alone or in a Coalition) simply means *living with the BJP/ Sangh*. It is no recipe whatever for destroying the latter or decisively undermining its overall influence, although it may of course please those who want a stable pro-capitalist order where two sides that don't differ too much from each other compete periodically for state power.

B. It is still a fact that, objectively speaking, the continental size and incredible cultural diversity and social complexity of the country creates real and powerful obstacles for Hindutva's homogenizing project. So put one's faith not on any of these failed and failing parties but on the still many progressive peoples and social movements that continue to exist and dot the Indian landscape in so many places. Here the crucial question becomes how can they be connected? The one major effort to do this–the National Alliance of People's Movement (NAPM) set up in 1992–has been very limited in its overall political and electoral impact. There are other reasons for believing that, contra Manuel Castells, a 'network of networks' is not the organisational path that will bring about a dramatic social and democratic transformation.[5]

C. One of the weak spots of Hindutva, it is said, is caste. So creating a unity of Dalits with the lower and most backward sections of the OBCs is crucial. Once established, this will be the hub around which other oppressed sections can coalesce. Lower caste rather than working class unity is the key. It is true that since the late 1980s there has been Dalit and lower caste assertion, but it is important to understand why this has not been a serious barrier to the growth of Hindutva once the Sangh accepted reservation policies for the OBCs as well as for Dalits and Adivasis. Talk of this caste assertion being nothing less than a 'second democratic revolution' was always misleading.

   Given the enormous sub-caste divisions among Dalits and among OBCs, the formation of caste blocs to assert themselves is always partial and limited, excluding other sub-castes within the Dalit and OBC fold. The upper ranks led most OBC mobilisations and Mayawati's BSP reflected the dominance within Dalits of the Jatavs or Chamars of UP. In Maharashtra the main Dalit Republican Party of India (RPI) has relied predominantly on the Mahar sub-caste. The aim of these caste assertions was to rise up. This did not mean becoming a higher caste or sub-caste (those older patterns of behaviour through what has been called Sanskritisation, i.e. emulating the beliefs and practices of those higher up) but seeking to improve one's status and existing position in three key respects–achieving a stronger sense of dignity by getting greater respect or recognition; materially improving one's condition; and finally, getting hold of the levers of political power. To do this there had to be coalitions with other, including higher, castes and their representative parties. Despite all references to the inspiration provided by Ambedkar, the political leadership among Dalits and also political representatives of the lower most deprived rungs within the OBCs never sought to unite, let alone to mobilise, to overthrow the caste system. Rather, it was and is to rise within the caste framework.

For Ambedkar, Hinduism and the caste system was an inseparable whole hence Dalit escape from, but not destruction of, the caste system could be accomplished through the abandonment of Hinduism and conversion to Buddhism. It is most revealing that the proportion of such neo-Buddhists since Ambedkar's conversion has remained very small and roughly stable. Most Dalits and lower castes have not converted to Buddhism but have remained within the Hindu fold and are thus very open to messages espousing Hindu pride as well as sharing common sentiments that scapegoat Muslims for personal insecurities. Meanwhile, those sub-castes at the bottom rungs of either the Dalits or the OBCs which have not benefited from this 'second democratic revolution' have been resentful respectively of those sub-castes among Dalits and those among the OBCs who have monopolised placements provided through the reservations policy in education and government, making them easy fodder for the Sangh. In the latest elections, some 65 per cent of the constituencies where only Dalits and Tribals stood as candidates, the victors belonged to the BJP. There has also been a significant Hindutva-isation of the OBCs.

D. What then about the existing Indian Left? Do the mainstream Left parties, the Communist Party of India (CPI) and the Communist Party of India-Marxist (CPI-M), remain the only hope? The less said about this view the better. Long reduced to being primarily an electoral force with a diminishing cadre base that clings to old Stalinist verities when it does think about Marxism, their cadres with a few exceptions in some pockets, have lost the capacity and interest in pursuing the politics of popular mobilisation around genuine and justified grievances of ordinary people. Collectively, these two parties secured one seat in Kerala, and four seats in Tamil Nadu, thanks largely to their pre-poll alliance with the DMK.

The parliamentary Left has long lost the capacity to relate to working class struggles. Left governments in West Bengal, Kerala and Tripura, carried out occasional mass mobilisations for electoral purposes or for preserving their control where challenged by other forces or parties. Since 1991, there have been continuous assaults on the working class. Left TUs have responded with periodic (17) general strikes to show their anger, resulting in a temporary rise in their popularity. But there has been no serious or sustained work to rebuild unions, organise contract workers, or help in a non-manipulative way progressive social struggles and movements not under their control or leadership.

The cadres and activists of this parliamentary Left are not of the same calibre as those of the late 70s, when this Left, led by the CPM, rose to power in West Bengal and later in Tripura. There has, subsequently, been a steady degeneration whereby the material and status gains for cadres and activists through patronage, increasingly became the primary reason for their loyalty. Similarly, it made most sense for its voter base to support the party/front most likely to win in the Lok Sabha, assembly and panchayat elections. This pattern of behaviour was reinforced in places by the presence of lumpenised cadre that could threaten challengers and provide protection for the 'faithful'. Since 2006 there has been a steady decline of the Left in eastern India at all electoral levels. Kerala's Left decline has been slower because governmental alternation after each assembly election had forced the party to periodically behave as a pro-people's militant opposition.

The collapse of the Soviet Union and the capitalist turn in China only accelerated the ideological disarray among the members of this Left. Domestic political-ideological decay has, however, remained the primary factor. Ironically, the key strategic perspective retained unswervingly from the Stalinist era has been 'popular frontism' with bourgeois parties. Electorally, this has required unprincipled compromises in Kerala as well as nationally. Not surprisingly, extra-parliamentary mass mobilisation and the building of an ever expanding mass base as self-inoculation against internal degeneration, has long been relegated as the key route to promoting radical politics.

What then of the ML movement? The most serious challenge to the Indian state was presented by the underground Maoist movement although split into various factions/parties. Even after partial unification the biggest of these, the ML People's War Group, is now on a progressively downward slide, losing cadres and leaders, along with a shrinking geographical presence. The ML more generally has two key structural problems. One is its understanding of India as a semi-feudal and semi-colonial power, which results in its justification of the disastrous strategic pathway of 'countryside surrounding the cities'. The second problem is that the structures created for long-term underground struggle have their own dynamic of operation. This has enabled the accumulation of necessary finances creating vested interests. At the same time, necessarily decentralised armed squadrons take on a life of their own with often different backward and forward linkages of support and activity that even sometimes lead to intra-organisation clashes for territorial control.

It is not as if there is no awareness among the leaders of such ML groups of these problems. But given how ML groups have either faded away or become much weaker in terms of political influence once they have surfaced and abandoned the underground struggle, there is not much incentive for the others to follow that route. In short, the ML movement is caught in a strategic-organisational trap from which it does not know how to escape. However much one might respect the sacrifices and commitment of its activists, ML politics is a dead-end.

E. The last and, to my mind, the only realistic option is the creation of a new, much more radical Left force through a process which for a long time will be one of molecular accumulation, but also through splits and fusions among existing left forces, and in particular conjunctures of more dramatic popular upheaval can achieve a growth that is much more sudden and dramatic. Collectively over time such struggles can achieve a critical mass that ensures a more enduring stability of presence. Central to this process will be the development of ideologically trained and disciplined cadres involved in concrete struggles on multiple fronts and guided by a larger transformative vision of building a capitalism-transcending socialism, whose democratic character will be much deeper than anything capitalist liberal democracy can hope to provide. The struggle to destroy the hegemonising drive of Hindutva cannot be separated from this counter-transformative project of building democratic socialism. If this sounds completely fanciful, it is not–for two reasons, one both national and international, the other, specifically Indian.

First, contemporary capitalism is not capable of resolving three life threatening problems which because they are so serious will always generate widespread and growing anger and concern and therefore activisms at a mass level that can and must be integrated and channelized to become a powerful transformative force. (i) There will continue to be mass deprivations with the denial of basic needs such as health, education, public housing and transport, pensions, etc., concurrent with the most shameful levels of inequality of income and wealth though there is no global scarcity of resources to eliminate such deprivations for all. Much below the level of what we now consider basic needs, there are those who are malnourished and under-nourished and whose number globally is around 2 billion, of which India has the disproportionately single largest share. (ii) The capitalist despoliation of the environment is damaging in unforeseen ways the delicate balance in the relationship between the global eco-system and the living patterns of the human species. (iii) The dark clouds threatening nuclear war remain in the firmament even as the locations over which they cast a shadow may shift.

The second reason specific to India is that up and down the country, there is the presence of various groups and independent activists involved in various progressive struggles who still see themselves as radical and revolutionary leftists, even as they have through their own experiences become relatively disillusioned with the hitherto two dominant traditions of the Indian Left–Stalinism and Maoism.

There is therefore fertile ground to plough and we need to get on with it.

Notes

1. "Not Just Lavasa's Wife, His Sister and Son Also Under I-T Department's Scanner", September 25, 2019 at thewire.in
2. See Maninder Dabas, "84 Activists Killed, Many More Are Missing Or Threatened: Now The RTI Itself Is Under Threat", July 28, 2019 at indiatimes.com
3. For a summary assessment of its key conclusions and their wider implications see the Appendix.
4. Shivshankar Menon, *Choices: Inside the Making of India's Foreign Policy*, Penguin Random House, India, 2016, pp. 164-165.
5. See the next chapter on "The Question of Organisation".

5

The Question of Organisation: Beyond Marx, the Enduring Legacy of Lenin

The 'Organisation question' necessarily devolves into two others—'Organisation for What'? 'Organisation by Whom'? Let us declare that our goal is to carry out in perhaps the very long term, the project of dramatically reducing, even seeking to completely eliminate, various human relations of oppression and exploitation while establishing an ecologically stable balance between human society and nature. Then how are we to go about this given that our current context is marked by a dynamic and interacting economic-political duality of a capitalist process of globalization and a persistent multiple nation-states system? Since the nation-state is and will remain for the foreseeable future the most important political unit, progressive transformations in some major countries are almost certainly necessary to kick-start and accelerate the desired transformation at the global level.

Socialism or Democracy

But what is this transformative goal that we seek? Classically, the name given to this by the International Left was 'Socialism', meaning the transcending of the capitalist order. Today those still seeing themselves as belonging to the Left are much more divided. Some have come to terms permanently with capitalism believing that the only realistic goal is to strive for a more humane and green capitalist order. This essay, however, is concerned with that more radical part of the Left which still believes that it is necessary and possible to transcend capitalism but which is itself divided about how central capitalism is to the sustenance and further consolidation of the wider web of oppressive relations and therefore what importance to be given to the classical understanding and pursuit of Socialism and Revolution.

There are Marxists, and some who while seeing themselves as post-Marxists or ex-Marxists, do recognize that going beyond capitalism is the necessary but not sufficient condition for achieving wider and deeper emancipation. But now basic perspectives diverge. Marxists will still talk the language of Socialist Revolution as both process and event–the latter as a decisive turning point in the pursuit of wider emancipation. Most post- or ex-Marxists who nevertheless continue to politically position themselves on the radical left, will be much more inclined to designate the final goal as Democracy (with a capital D) that is said to subsume the socialist project itself. In contrast to those Marx-inspired socialists–be they Stalinist, Maoist, Trotskyist or from other left-libertarian traditions, who see class struggle and politics as the primary route towards achieving the final goal of comprehensive emancipation–they would insist there must be no privileging of the working class as the main harbinger of liberation. Rather, there must be equal respect for what multiple actors, each fighting against their own vectors of oppression, can bring to the collective effort. Capitalism, they would aver, is but one vector among other such vectors, all interacting with each other in complex ways and with variable outcomes.

For such ex- or post-Marxists, the corollary of giving undue emphasis to the role of the working class is to give undue emphasis to the economic structure of capitalism in the shaping of contemporary human societies when due weight they aver must also be given to other sources of power be these in the domains of politics, law, technology, culture or ideology. Indeed, the very notion of power itself must be rethought in the light of new insights since coercion itself has many sources and takes many forms, not only or primarily of armed violence of which the state has an unmatched capacity to exercise. Though the sources of power over us have material bases, they would not have the power they have if we did not internalise the subjective evaluations associated with identities that are socially imposed on us through processes of 'classification' and identification. Class struggle then involves the de-stabilising of these 'social markers of power'; and this newer understanding of 'class struggle' means it is not a concept that can be confined to the working class alone but is being carried out by all oppressed groups.

Insofar as there is a wider 'structure of power' it is said to be much looser and diffuse and the way to overcome it is through a much looser form of overlapping networks of struggles waged by different identity formations none to be privileged over the other. Where there are authoritarian regimes the popular desire that is paramount is to establish a liberal democratic polity. In already existing capitalist liberal democracies, the path towards the goal of a 'Radical, Pluralist Democracy' is to be more sensibly seen as gradualist and cumulative and not to be fixated on some supposedly decisive point of confrontation with state power.

A Critique

Before discussing the strategic issue of how to transcend capitalism we need to be clear about the relationship of capitalist social relations to (a) democracy and (b) to other oppressive relations such as those of caste, hetero-normative patriarchy, race, etc. Capitalism is the first social order that by significantly separating the economic and the political *permits* the possible emergence of a new kind of civic political equality for *all* (unlike Athenian democracy) since the extraction and realisation of economic surplus can now take place within the economic realm of market relations without the use or threat of use of politically constituted power on a 'free' labour force. This allows for the first time the emergence of a ruling class that need not be directly governing and a labour force juridically and politically free from personal dependence but *compelled* on pain of survival to offer itself for hire on the market. The politics of production (the workplace) and the politics of coercion (the state) are separated. Of course 'allowing' is not the same as enabling–it has taken struggles over time and from below by working classes, women, people of colour and the lower castes to make liberal democracy and the formal political equality of citizens a reality.

No other structure of oppression–caste-ism, racism, patriarchy–allows or permits as a result of its *very nature* the emergence of key aspects/features/characteristics of democracy in the modern sense of the term. One way of grasping what this means is to perceive that the interaction between capitalist social relations and all other oppressive relations is asymmetric. The reshaping capacity of capitalist relations on others is significantly greater than vice versa, though this does not mean that it necessarily absorbs other social relations since given the uneven and combined character of capitalist development, all kinds of social, political and cultural hybrids and admixtures can and do emerge in ways unimaginable in the pre-capitalist past. Capitalism possesses a *distinctive flexibility* vis-a-vis other forms of oppression, a flexibility that allows relative to the past, for considerable advances in the generation of greater social and political equalities for women, non-whites, sexual minorities, and lower castes. So much so, that many Afro-Americans and Latinos in the US, important and powerful currents within feminism and LGBTQI movements worldwide, as well as sections among Dalits and Adivasis in India are deluded into believing that the persistence of capitalism is compatible with–and for some even necessary for–the steady and continuous deepening of democracy and the erosion of debilitating social relations.

The problem is that this remarkable flexibility of capitalist social relations is inseparable from a profound and inescapable inflexibility–the necessary persistence of unequal, unjust and, above all, *exploitative* class relations without which capitalism itself cannot survive.[1] There are fundamental limits to the extent to which class inequalities of income, wealth, status and power can diminish let alone disappear and therefore limits are imposed on how democratic the polity can be. In short, a capitalist liberal democracy must remain capitalist! The questions that therefore face both the acolytes of Radical Democracy and Marxists are twofold? How to transcend capitalism? How to unite all oppressed and exploited categories? These in turn segue into two other key issues. First, how are we to understand the nature and distribution of power, in particular the question of state power? Second, what is the organisational form that must be developed for unifying the various struggles waged by the oppressed and the exploited? Should we adopt a pluralist and network form of organisation or a 'network of networks' as our supporters of Radical Democracy might argue? Or do we need–as the crucial mechanism(s)–the construction of a radical party or set of parties? And if the latter, what kind of radical or revolutionary party or set of parties do we need?

It is precisely here that the crucial importance of Lenin emerges and whose insights and practice continues to provide enduring lessons for us today and tomorrow.

Lenin and the Vanguard Party

Lenin, like Marx, provided no theory of the party but he did provide crucial insights still valid for helping to construct the organisational form capable of overthrowing the capitalist state. Marx didn't always distinguish party from the working class movement as a whole but flirted between two stands either seeing the working class itself as the historical party thrown up by capitalism or the party as a separate political body but *subordinated* to the working class. There is a fundamental discontinuity between Marx and Lenin. It is Lenin who perceived the necessity of building a revolutionary party *of* but not *in* the working class neither separated from, nor dissolved within, but in constant interaction with the working class movement. The proper expression of this key principle is the *vanguard* party or organisation.

But if vanguardism has received a very bad press from Western Cold War historians and intellectuals, it has also been seen by many on the anti-Leninist left as the 'original sin' responsible for the degeneration into Stalin's brutal one party authoritarianism. For Stephen Kotkin who is a relatively recent entrant into the ranks of Western right wing anti-Soviet historians, Marxism led to Bolshevism/Leninism which led to Stalinism. But two historians of the left, writing in the 2017 issue of the *Economic and Political Weekly* commemorating the Russian Revolution, hold views not that different. For Dilip Simeon, Leninism shaped Bolshevism and led to Stalinism while for Marcel Van Der Linden, Leninism led to Stalinism but there was a chasm between Lenin's ideas about organisation and Bolshevik organisational practice.[2]

The central reference point for both detractors and supporters of Lenin's thinking on the problem of organisation is, of course, *What Is To Be Done?* (WITBD?). For detractors this where you will find proof that Leninist vanguardism is so elitist because the text shows his contempt of the intelligence and therefore capacity of the working class to go beyond 'trade union consciousness'. Revolutionary consciousness–equated with theory–can only be brought to the class by middle class intellectuals and 'injected', as it were, to create the desired vanguard party.

Defenders of Lenin's understanding as laid down in WITBD? do so along two paths that partly overlap. There is a detailed scrutiny of the text itself to show how detractors have seriously misrepresented the meaning and wrongly belittled the meaning and value of Lenin's concept of vanguard organisation; and also the failure to situate the text properly in the general political circumstances of the time (1902) when it was written. This second line of defence is best exemplified by the very title of Lars Lih's remarkable book, *Lenin Rediscovered: 'What Is To Be Done?' in Context.*[3]

The great importance of Lih's work is that it is now the most exhaustive and comprehensive demolition of the foundational assumption of what he calls the 'textbook interpretation' of WITBD? held by Western Cold War warriors and left anti-Leninists–which is of Lenin's deep 'worry about workers' as presumably expressed in his views on 'spontaneity' and 'consciousness'.[4] The organisational logic that is postulated in such a stance towards workers is then said to lead to Lenin's promotion of a highly centralised, authoritarian (or at best paternalist) structure whose top layers manipulate the social base. This deliberately constructed vanguard structure is then said to be responsible more than anything else (there are other 'secondary' factors) for the emergence of a dynamic wherein the party substitutes for the class, the intellectual leadership for the party rank-and-file and ultimately the individual 'dictator' for the leadership bodies since unavoidable disputes about policy and courses of action will repeatedly surface and will require a 'neutral arbiter who stands above all others' to finally adjudicate. Leninism led to Stalinism and to Soviet 'totalitarianism'.

The centrepiece of the assault on Leninist vanguardism, indeed its sum and substance, is to be found in the following two quotes from WITBD?[5]

1. "We have said *there could not have been* Social Democratic consciousness among the workers. It would have to be brought to them from without. The history of all countries shows that the working class exclusively by its own efforts, is able to develop only trade union consciousness.....The theory of socialism, however, grew out of the philosophic, historical and economic theories elaborated by educated representatives of the propertied classes, by intellectuals."[6]

   Some pages later, Lenin quotes a long passage directly taken from Kautsky from which this part is taken and presented here:

2. ".....Socialism and the class struggle arise side by side and not one out of the other; they arise out of different conditions. Modern socialist consciousness can arise only on the basis of profound scientific knowledge..... The vehicle of science is not the proletariat but the bourgeois intelligentsia..... Thus socialist consciousness is something introduced into the proletariat's class struggle from without and not something that arose from it spontaneously....."[7]

A Basic Misreading

For Lih it is above all the failure, or perhaps refusal, to understand the conjuncture during which WITBD? was written (1902) that explains the misreading of Lenin's general attitude towards the working class and his polemics against other political currents therein. This was a context of a strong upsurge of struggles from the mid-1890s onwards and rising hopes for radical change from Tsarism. Hence WITBD?'s political thrust towards the urgent need to prepare to take advantage of *forthcoming opportunities*. Far from bemoaning the working class he was appealing to those who considered themselves to be revolutionaries and in radical groups. It is not just that Lenin (like many others) proved prescient about the likelihood of a future crisis which did erupt in 1905 but that only then can one, as Lih has shown, make proper sense of Lenin, his differences with other currents from the Economists to the Mensheviks and even within the Bolsheviks where he was consistently more confident and trusting about the potential of the working class and the willingness of its vanguard to move forward.

But how does this explain the failure of detractors to read the text of WITBD? with due deliberation and thoughtfulness? This is being written when Lenin perceives a great "awakening of the masses (principally the industrial proletariat) in that its weakness lies in the lack of consciousness and initiative among the revolutionary leaders."[8] Passages in WITBD? repeatedly make this point. "Revolutionaries however *lagged behind* this upsurge; both in their 'theories' and in their activity...."[9] Or "...both the terrorist and Economists *underestimate* the revolutionary activity of the masses....both fail to devote sufficient attention to the development of *their own activity* in political agitation and in the organisation of exposures..."[10] Again, "....And they will come to us....only when... we represent a *political force*....In order to become such a force in the eyes of outsiders, much persistent and stubborn work is required *to raise* our own consciousness, initiative and energy...."[11] Even more decisively, "It shows that we were right in our opinion that the principal cause of the present crisis in Russian Social Democracy is the *lag of the leaders* ('ideologists, revolutionaries, Social Democrats) behind the *spontaneous upsurge of the masses...*"[12] Clearly, the attribution to Lenin of believing that revolutionary consciousness is equivalent to theoretical knowledge is mistaken. So what is the role of theory? Here Lenin endorses Kautsky's view that socialist theory and ideology comes from outside the class. This is a reference to the origins of socialist doctrine which is the basis for the *worldview* whose key *message* or 'mission statement' is of the working class's historical role as the strategic agent that *can* and *should* overthrow the capitalist state and usher in a new era.[13] Or as Alan Shandro points out, theory is crucial for recognizing and sustaining the belief or view or perspective that the respective class interests of the bourgeoisie and working class are *irreconcilable* in capitalism and hence opening the working class to the practical implications and actions that follow from this.[14] The revolutionary party moreover is the collective that must act as the ongoing *memory* of the class and the *preserver* of the lessons learnt from past struggles and this requires analysis, debate and study so that the party programme is created and constantly updated. It is the programme that makes the party (not vice-versa) and makes it the instrument dedicated to fulfilling certain tasks flowing from that programme.

The practical injunction in WITBD? was that the paper *Iskra*'s primary responsibility was not to be a theoretical journal—contrary to this being the supposed pathway to developing and spreading revolutionary consciousness through propaganda—but to concentrate on *political exposure* of all kinds to promote agitation on various fronts among various sections of the oppressed, and not to focus primarily on economic and industrial issues of struggle.[15] Why? What then is the process by which a revolutionary vanguard can emerge? And what then is the meaning of a vanguard if it is not to be primarily a bunch of middle class intellectuals whose forte is theory?

The Real Process

It is quite extraordinary that all the detractors relying in large part or whole on WITBD? for their 'injection thesis' have either never registered, or what is worse have deliberately ignored, the fact that Lenin uses the 'from without' formula in two different ways. The first much cited by them is Lenin's endorsement of the Kautsky passage regarding theory. But it is the second usage that lies at the heart of Lenin's understanding of how revolutionary consciousness emerges and develops; why there is the necessity of forming a vanguard organisation; and what the relationship of the party to the class should be. Indeed, the whole thrust of WITBD? culminating in its practical injunction to carry out (through *Iskra*) 'political exposure', follows directly from this second sense of the 'from without' formula.

In the section aptly and significantly subtitled 'The Working Class as Vanguard Fighter For Democracy', Lenin writes the following: "....Economists commit namely their conviction that it is possible to develop the class political consciousness of the workers *from within* so to speak from their economic struggle, i.e. by making this struggle the exclusive (or at least the main) starting point, by making it the exclusive (or at least the main) basis. Such a view is radically wrong....Class political consciousness can be brought to the workers *only from without*, that is only from outside the sphere of relations between workers and employers. The sphere from which alone it is possible to obtain this knowledge is the sphere of relationships of all classes and strata to the state and government, the sphere of the interrelations between *all* classes....to bring political knowledge to the *workers* the Social Democrats must *go among all classes of the population*; they must dispatch units of their army in all directions."[16]

What Lenin is saying is profoundly important. Revolutionary consciousness must try and be much more encompassing and cannot emerge from a sectional or partial perspective on society, from the lessons of only partial and sectional struggles. As Norman Geras rightly put it: "The sphere from which alone it is possible to obtain this knowledge is the sphere of relationship to *all* classes and strata to the state and government the sphere of the interrelations between *all* classes. 'Inside' and 'outside' in this passage refer not now to sociological groupings, as it were, workers and bourgeois intellectuals......They refer instead respectively to the partial and the global. Socialist consciousness is not generated out of any particular struggle. No such struggle leads automatically towards an adequate understanding. This can come only from a global perspective on the relations between all classes."[17]

No single individual can embody this wider and more encompassing consciousness. This is a vision of the party as above all a 'political centraliser' of fragmentary struggles, sectional experiences and partial perspectives of different layers of the masses in order ultimately to confront the 'politically centralising instance' of bourgeois society, the bourgeois state! This is a conception of the revolutionary as a "*tribune of the people*, who is able to react to every manifestation of tyranny and oppression, no matter what stratum and class of people it affects...."[18] This is the task of the party since "working class consciousness cannot be genuine political consciousness unless workers are trained to respond to all cases of tyranny, oppression and abuse, no matter *what class* is affected..."[19] This is also the only way for the working class to try and exercise hegemony over other social groups such as the peasantry and sections of the petty bourgeoisie or middle layers that are contradictorily located within class relations.[20]

The Vanguard Party and Democratic Centralism

There is one huge dilemma and another awkward embarrassment for those on the radical left who take their distance from Lenin. First, insofar as they hail the Russian Revolution as an historic step forward (no matter how much responsibility they might assign to Lenin for subsequent degeneration of party and state) his intervention at a crucial juncture in the October Days was decisive for ensuring its success. How did the 'elitist' and 'vanguardist' party of Lenin and the Bolsheviks grow so quickly and become as big as it did between February and October 1917. Here, a widely held view in such circles is that it did so by betraying, not following, Leninist principles while Lenin himself was a master opportunist who somehow 'seized the time'. The other embarrassment is that in this hectic period of upheavals in 1917, Lenin is writing what for these circles would be the most 'anti-Leninist' and 'anti-authoritarian' text which barely mentions the party, namely *State and Revolution*.[21] Yet the explanation is simple, straightforward and in tune with the character of virtually all his political writings–it was practically motivated by the political needs and emergencies of the time. On the verge of possible seizure of power there had to be some blueprint, no matter how rough, for constructing the new proletarian state.

This essay however is focused on Lenin 'out of power' for whom the central issue was forging the mechanism for challenging and seizing state power–the vanguard party. To talk of a vanguard is simply to talk of the necessity of leadership. The direction taken by any mass movement is never decided by the *average* consciousness of its mass following but by that of its leading elements or layer.[22] There is always an uneven spread of consciousness in the working class. Gramsci talked of the worker's 'stretched' or 'contradictory' consciousness. The working class is pulled in two opposing directions. Its experience of exploitation and oppression pushes it towards socialism but the reality of bourgeois dominance including of ruling class ideas and efforts at hegemony pulls it away from the ideas, hopes and struggles for socialism. Here, it is not the socialisation and deep internalisation of the mores and values of the dominant culture that is the biggest barrier for the development of revolutionary consciousness. That would suggest that the key terrain of struggle must itself be cultural. Rather, it is the seeming absence of a radical alternative to the existing order, i.e., not cultural consensus or the worker's 'false consciousness' but the *lack* of a 'unified dissensus' that is the greatest barrier.[23] This is why when unexpectedly after a long hiatus there is a sudden mass eruption of struggle on various fronts–the coming together of both the politics of the singular and the politics of the universal (which historically has taken the forms of nationalism, democracy, socialism separately or in some combination)–that mass revolutionary consciousness rises by leaps and bounds. This invariably causes the sometimes dramatic re-composition of the vanguard as many earlier more advanced elements fall back while newer elements race past them in pursuit of newer possibilities and tasks.[24] What happened in 1917 Russia and in so many revolutionary upsurges since, is proof enough that this dynamic holds.

The vanguard is never a *fixed* sociological category but always a *relational* one to the broader masses. The members of the vanguard are the dedicated 'shock troops' on the 'front lines' of a struggle waged by a much wider body. The self-emancipation of the working class *requires* leadership. Do not counterpose self-activity to vanguardism. The vanguard party seeks to *combine* the highest levels of consciousness with the highest levels of worker self-activity and self-organisation because the two do not come together automatically or as separately interacting streams. There can be high levels of class activity but low levels of class consciousness and vice versa.[25]

It is in fact absurd to make no difference between a 'vanguard' and 'elite'. The former is a *specific* category, the latter a more general one having not specific knowledge, understanding or capabilities but simply more *social power* and 'higher' social status. So there are several kinds of vanguards, e.g. those having medical, artistic or even athletic skills rather than political knowledge and skills of practice. Moreover, political vanguards can dissolve away as the tasks to which they are geared are achieved. But vanguards can also 'petrify' into elites. So it is always an open question whether this happens, *not* one that is pre-determined by the fact of being a vanguard.[26]As for the much maligned notion of Democratic Centralism much of the existing left parties of Stalinist or Maoist persuasion or historical inspiration have failed to understand that it is not an organisational dictum but above all a *political* concept with variable organisational embodiments. As Ernest Mandel, one of the main leaders of the Fourth International put it "Centralization is not to be taken in the first place as an organizational dimension, and in no way whatsoever is it essentially an administrative one. It is political........It means *centralization of experience, centralization of knowledge, centralization of conclusions* drawn out of actual militancy."[27] This is of course, the only way a vanguard party or formation can generate the necessary wider consciousness to challenge the crucial vanguard formation of its bourgeois enemies–the *bourgeois state*. Given the unavoidable competition between capitals and the separation of the economic and political in capitalism, it is above all the state–that through its own mechanisms of centralising knowledge of different sections of the population and of differences and divergences within the ruling class bloc–can best arbitrate over intra- and inter-class tensions as well as be the strongest protector of the interests, position and power of the ruling class bloc.

It is for this reason that Lenin called state power the central question posed by the revolutionary project.

The Question of Dual Power

Lenin's classic formula for when the 'Revolution as Event' becomes possible, is when the ruling classes can no longer rule in the old way and when the ruled are no longer willing to be so ruled i.e. when the state is in *grave* crisis and the *possibility* of a breakthrough to a new kind of state becomes *visible*. In the unfolding of this process there are two phases with no automatic transition from the first to the second. There is first the emergence of a crisis situation when, for reasons that may well have nothing or little to do with the activism of revolutionary forces, key apparatuses of the state can no longer function as in normal times. The possibility of revolutionary change i.e. of changing the existing class character of the state, becomes real. This may come from the breakdown of the army as in First World War Tsarist Russia or in the fall of Caetano's dictatorship in Portugal in 1974 as middle and some upper ranks of the officer corps were radicalised by the anti-colonial national liberation wars in Portuguese Africa. It may come from massive state disruption by the quite unexpectedly huge mass mobilisations as in the overthrow of the Shah of Iran in 1979 or of Mubarak in Egypt in 2011.[28]

Precisely because the state is in crisis that there arise 'embryonic organs of dual power', so called because they are structures arising from below that are subjected to more direct forms of popular control wresting power from their employers, as in the industrial belts or 'cordones' of 1970-73 Chile or in the 'shoras' of Iranian oil workers in 1979. An even stronger dual power challenge was presented by workers and soldiers councils or Soviets, whose very functioning undermined state authority and legitimacy. There has also been the second much more prolonged situation of dual power contestation, namely the Chinese and Vietnamese Communist-led revolutions based on militarily 'liberated zones' and the presence of alternative structures of state-society there. Such dual power situations cannot last for very long. There will have to be a resolution of this crisis situation in one direction or the other. Here is where the second phase comes in—when there are revolutionary forces which recognise and take on the crucial task of actually confronting existing state power to change its social character in a decisive test of strength; where the question of 'who wins?' is posed and answered one way or the other? For Lenin a vanguard body of some significant strength must be there when this kind of crisis situation erupts and if there is to be a forward movement to the 'final showdown' this vanguard layer must *fuse* with the majority of the working class which alone with the support of allies can carry out the revolution. Taking power is an event—a matter of *decision* and *timing* where time is itself a political factor.

The late Daniel Bensaid expressed it neatly when he said that for Lenin politics was "conceived as the art of unexpected events....."[29] Lenin's politics is about 'strategy' so identifying the strategically important actors for and against; seizing 'favourable moments'; attacking the 'weak links'—all this is in stark contrast to Kautsky's approach of passive accumulation of forces.

But can we still talk of dual power situations emerging in our times? Clearly, one form of dual power and the strategy associated with it cannot be replicated. The Chinese, Vietnamese and Yugoslav revolutions took place in economically backward societies where it was the fusion of nationalism and socialism that was the main source of mass support. With very few exceptions, if any, that era of armed struggles for national liberation is over. Moreover, capitalist states have learnt their own lessons from the past. Even smaller states can now exercise much higher levels of ruthless repression either on their own or can count on military support and even intervention from stronger countries against domestic revolutionary forces seeking to emulate the successes of China, Vietnam, Yugoslavia or even Cuba. And what path to follow when it comes to capitalist liberal democracies albeit those which, democratically speaking, are quite flawed? So far there has been no successful socialist revolution in such states.

Here, the first kind of near dual power situation remains not just a plausible possibility but has, in weaker and stronger forms, resurfaced from time to time. This was the case with Portugal and Chile in the 1970s and in Poland in the early 1980s. In Iran and Portugal significant forces committed to socialism existed but missed the opportunity to forge ahead. Chile provided a negative lesson by the Allende government assuming that in a decades-long constitutional democracy where the army had hitherto remained aloof from the civilian government, it would never carry out a coup to prevent socialist advance. In Poland, Solidarity, the strongest and most united working class organisation ever, lost its way because its leadership insisted that its revolution was "self-limiting", i.e. Solidarity would not seek state power but would bypass the state to transform society–the end result was military rule in 1983.

Such crisis situations carrying a powerful dynamic and potential for rapid revolutionary change will emerge as ruling classes everywhere, beholden as they are to either disciplinary or compensatory forms of neoliberal capitalism, cannot prevent the guaranteed emergence of wider and deeper mass discontent. But can the forces for radical socialist transformation seize the opportunities that will emerge? Revolutionary vanguard organisations must achieve a significant implantation *prior* to such upheavals which can emerge anywhere including in the advanced capitalist democracies. Today, there are many countries that have elected parliaments, multi-party competition and some modicum level of civil liberties even as it is an ongoing struggle to maintain let alone extend these freedoms and rights. Revolutionary forces in these countries are always cadre-based organisations where ideological training and commitment alongside activism by its cadres is a must if they are to survive and grow. To have an electoral and parliamentary presence is necessary, and to want to come to power at the provincial and central levels is fine. But seeing how such one-time forces have become tamed through involvement in electoral politics it is vital to absorb certain historical lessons.

1. Extra-parliamentary activism by cadres on *all* fronts–the essence of what it means to build a vanguard layer and

body—is not only the key to expanding the influence of the far-left party or formation but also the best way to enhance its parliamentary strength.

2. The only *realistic* long term strategy for the far left today is to fight for the progressive accumulation of reforms. Do not counter-pose reforms to revolution but understand the relation between them. Here, the bridge is provided by what has been called the *Transitional Programme* of demands and the struggles around them. These demands are of different kinds and *many* of the reforms therein, especially those aiming to reduce corporate power of command, are known as 'revolutionary reforms' or 'anti-capitalist structural reforms'. Some of these are highlighted in the demands given below.
    (i) For civic and human rights.
    (ii) Social democratic demands for basic livelihood needs. When these are met it generates greater confidence; and when unmet this raises awareness about the limitations in the existing order thereby promoting efforts to think and go beyond it.
    (iii) Those demands whose fulfilment erodes bourgeois power and property such as workers control/wage indexation/opening of company books/institutional and industrial democracy which in turn promotes worker/citizen self-organisation.
    (iv) Promoting cooperative forms of production and distribution thereby creating shared spaces of de-commodification and hence a practical awareness of what a non-capitalist more socialist form of the economy might look like.
    (v) Struggles for a 'right to the city/locality'. This is an important way to bring about greater unity among the various sections of working masses since it would address their common collective needs where they live. But such struggles are usually directed against the state for fulfilling demands. It is important to remember

that important though these are, it is the struggle at the workplace that hits the capitalist class where it hurts the most–at the point of profit making.

Depending on the context these transitional demands can be (a) mainly propagandistic, (b) action/movement generating, (c) generating a revolutionary momentum.

3. Forming fronts with other parties and organisations is a necessity. This is a *practical* unity which can be at the level of a single issue, a set of demands, at the level of a common struggle and even sometimes at the level of elections. But it is always a *tactical and carefully circumscribed* alliance where bourgeois or social democratic parties are concerned. One does not compromise on one's fundamental political principles and must always remain ideologically and organisationally independent.
4. When a party committed to socialism is in power at the local, regional or national levels, whether on its own or in a coalition, its main aim must not be to simply remain in power at all costs or to win successive election rounds because it believes it can be more reformist than the other parties when in power. That is the way to making unprincipled compromises and puts party governing ambitions first at the expense of class interests. The radical party's principal purpose when in government (at whatever level) is to carry out those actions and reforms that will promote, and help *institutionalise* greater working class self-organisation and power *outside* both the administration and the party itself. Only then can the working class in the broadest sense of the term be strengthened enough as to successively advance no matter which party the electoral roundabouts bring in.
5. Having already suggested this longer term strategy of accumulating reforms now comes an important warning. There remains the crucial issue of when does the trajectory of reformism shift into becoming the dynamic of revolution? Here the choice is between what might be called a 'Gateway' thesis and a 'Bastion' thesis. The first thesis claims that the

> only way to a revolutionary breakthrough is gradualist and non-violent; that the pathway is of first coming into central government, and even if there are occasions when the party retreats electorally, nevertheless through the process of revolutionary reformism over time (which may require repeated turns at governmental rule) the relationship of forces overall will be shifting more and more to the working class and its allies and against the ruling classes. So when the party or coalition once more comes to power and keeps pushing its project of change and transformation in all its forms within the state apparatuses, it will at some point have finally tipped the balancing scales of social power in its own favour. The forces of socialism will find themselves passing through the 'gateway' of central state power to the other side of a new kind of state where the transition can no longer be stalled or reversed by the class, administrative and political oppositions within the country.[30]

The 'bastion thesis' while agreeing with the necessity of striving for cumulative changes and acts of transformation in society and the state to progressively shift the balance of forces, insists that long before the 'peaceful' tipping point anticipated by the advocates of the 'gateway' argument arrives, there will be a sharp polarisation of the top echelons or bastions of the state apparatuses–the armed forces, the civil administration, the judiciary, the police–to the right and there will be a violent assault on the working class movement and revolutionary forces. Not only does this scenario find much greater empirical evidence in its favour, most notably where the gradualist effort to bring about socialism took place, namely in Allende's Chile, but bourgeois states in the advanced democracies, where the gateway strategy might appear to be the most appropriate, have not hesitated to use force against movements where the stakes are well short of struggling for systemic change, e.g. Macron today against the Yellow Vests. Furthermore, the bastion thesis enjoys a great advantage over its rival, for it *allows for and seeks to prepare* for the eventuality that the gateway thesis might fail and the worst-case scenario prevail. What this means is that there has to be a perspective of not just seeking to neutralise the armed forces by the counter-power of sustained mass mobilisation at the biggest scale possible but also a clear perspective of making demands pertaining to the needs of ordinary soldiers and police; to press for democratisation of their internal authority structures and to win over many of them to the revolutionary side. Again, unlike the gateway thesis, it is what is done outside rather than within the state that will prove decisive.

Lenin's legacy then remains an invaluable gift that we would be extremely foolish to disdain or debase.

Notes

1. For Marxists class is not simply a social marker of 'oppression' like other categories but a *relational* category of 'exploitation' and domination.
2. D. Simeon, "The Bolshevik Heritage" and MVD Linden, "Why Leninism and Bolshevism are Not the Same" both in *Economic and Political Weekly*, November 4, 2017; Simeon repeatedly cites S. Kotkin, (*Stalin: Paradoxes of Power 1878-1928*, Vol. I, Allen Lane, London, 2014) in support of his own arguments perhaps impressed by the latter's view that Stalin simply 'intensified the insanity inherent in Leninism'. Rightwing histories driven by Cold War mentalities can if sufficiently scholarly certainly provide important insights and analyses. But Kotkin's scholarship has been severely criticised. See in this respect Fred Williams, "A Review of Stephen Kotkin's 'Stalin: Paradoxes of Power 1878-1928'" at wsws.org and Tony Wood, "Lives of Jugashvili" in *New Left Review 95*, September-October 2015. Williams points out that Kotkin continues to hold to the highly discredited view that the 1917 Revolution was a coup, a "Bolshevik putsch" with minimal popular support; that given his zeal for linking Stalin and Lenin, Kotkin believes that Lenin's 'Last Testament' criticizing Stalin and the 'Addendum' calling for his removal as general secretary are forgeries. Wood says Kotkin repeatedly tries to minimize differences between Stalin and Lenin on a host of issues such as on federal structure, foreign trade, the Georgian affair. Moreover,

Kotkin also sees post-October 'capitalist encirclement' as a self serving myth. It was not the civil war that gives a push towards a dictatorship but the latter pushing towards the civil war! Wood goes so far as to indict Kotkin for "advancing tendentious claims on almost every one of its 950 pages." (*NLR 95*, p. 148).

3. Published by Brill, Leiden, 2006.
4. Simeon in his essay cited above shows no indication of having read Lih's book while Linden refers only to Lih's translation of two passages in WITBD? (one of which overlaps with the first quote given a few sentences later) but he does not at all engage with Lih's own arguments. Fortunately, two other presentations in the same issue of the *EPW*, November 4, 2017 by Alexander Rabinowitch and Kunal Chattopadhyay provide a partial but salutary corrective to Simeon and Linden.
5. Well before Lih highlighted these as the 'scandalous passages' that constituted the flimsy base for detractors, Norman Geras in an outstanding text had made the same point and cited these two extracts. See also my review article of Geras's *Literature and Revolution: Essays on Marxism* (Verso, London, 1986) titled 'In Defence of Leninism' in *Economic and Political Weekly*, September 13, 1986, which was specifically directed against left anti-Leninists in India wrongly critiquing WITBD? as the source-bed for later party and state degeneration.
6. *Lenin Selected Works*, Vol. 1, Progress Publishers, Moscow, 1975, p. 114.
7. Ibid., p. 121.
8. See my 'In Defence of Leninism', pp. 1639-1640.
9. *Selected Works*, p. 132.
10. Ibid, pp. 151-152.
11. Ibid., p. 161.
12. Ibid., p. 172. All italics in the above quotes are Lenin's.
13. A key difference between Kautsky and Lenin which Lih misses is that where Kautsky believed that the working class would carry out its historic task, Lenin never saw such certainty unfolding simply through a process of gradual accumulation of reforms. For Kautsky the revolutionary movement "cannot meet with

anything other than temporary defeats and must ultimately win." (K. Kautsky, *The Road to Power* in Chapter 1, Chicago, 1910). Later in Chapter 5 Kautsky writes "The Socialist party is a revolutionary party, but not a revolution-making party...It is no part of our work to instigate a revolution or to prepare the way for it....We know that the proletariat must continue to grow in numbers.... and that therefore its victory and the overthrow of capitalism, is inevitable."

14. Alan Shandro, *Lenin and the Logic of Hegemony: Political Theory in the Class Struggle*, Brill, Leiden, 2014, p. 145.
15. Because Linden (*EPW*, November 4, 2017, p. 77) believes that for Lenin, revolutionary consciousness had to be brought 'from without' by the intelligentsia, Linden has to claim that the main task of *Iskra* was 'propaganda' and the spreading of 'Social Democratic *ideas*' through political exposure. He is silent on why the focus of *Iskra* was not on theory. On p. 78 he says for Lenin the party had to be a "league of intellectuals".
16. *Selected Works*, pp. 152-153; Emphasis in the original. Since Lih has effectively demolished the 'worry over workers' assumption of Lenin's detractors he dismisses the substitutionist or elitist argument about the nature of the Bolshevik party. But he sees WITBD? as a faithful replication of Kautsky's Erfutian Programme with Lenin wanting to build a party like the German SPD, hence the struggle to overthrow autocracy and achieve political freedom, although Lenin also believed unlike other currents that it was possible and necessary to build a mass party even in underground conditions. Lih sees nothing original in the Leninist conception of the party and its relationship to the development of revolutionary consciousness because he does not register the importance of this passage developing the second sense of 'from without'. Lih refers to part of it only in a footnote on p. 646 of his huge tome dismissing it as an exception to Lenin's otherwise utter fealty to Kautsky on the party. See also Note 13 above. That Lenin may not have realized his own originality and break from Kautsky in respect of the party-class-masses relationship till 1914 or not even afterwards (See Lih, https://jacobinmag.com/2019/06/

karl-kautsky-vladimir-lenin-russian-revolution), is not important because his party-building endeavours before and after 1914 were quite different and in tune with his own vision of working class potential in relation to changing political tasks.

17. Geras, *Literature of Revolution*, p. 183.
18. *Selected Works*, p. 154.
19. Ibid., p. 145.
20. For an elaboration of 'contradictory class locations' see the works of the late Eric Olin Wright. For more on the Bolshevik search for hegemony, see A. Shandro, *Lenin and the Logic of Hegemony* and his chapter "Lenin and Hegemony: the Soviets, the Working Class and the Party in the Revolution of 1905", in S. Budgen, S. Kouvelakis, S. Zizek (eds.), *Lenin Reloaded: Towards a Politics of Truth*, Duke University Press, London, 2007.
21. One view is that this is an aberration and inexplicable since so unlike the 'true Lenin'. Another is that Lenin oscillated between anarchism and Jacobinism. This is the line taken by Simeon in 'The Bolshevik Heritage'. The most unusual line of attack is to blame not Lenin's concept of the party and WITBD? as the textual source of post-October authoritarianism but on his conception of the state whose source bed textually is *State and Revolution*. For a critique of this approach and other anti-Leninist shibboleths see my "Leninism, Socialist Democracy, Contemporary Problems" in *Economic and Political Weekly*, December 2, 1995.
22. In the biggest mass movement since independence in India–the Ram Janmabhoomi movement–the average consciousness of its supporters was that the mosque could remain but a Ram temple should be constructed there. But it was what the leading layer wanted more than anything else, namely the un-Constitutional destruction of the mosque that was the pre-determined goal, and outcome.
23. This is not to be confused with what has been advocated by the late Ernest Laclau and Chantal Mouffe, namely that all politics is necessarily populist and that there is a 'chain of equivalence' among all groups suffering from various forms of oppression. There is then, according to them and their admirers, no privileged

agency for achieving the goal of an emancipatory radical pluralist democracy. Then, to coalesce this diversity of feeling and anger requires the construction of a political discourse that expresses and unifies these diverse aspirations for which collective identification with a charismatic leader of the populist party-movement may be essential. What can unify this otherwise fragmented populace having differing concerns or interests must be what they are collectively against, i.e. the ruling dispensation. The 'people' must be posited against the 'elites'. In contrast, my emphasis on the issue of a non-unified dissensus, is meant as a critique of the 'dominant ideology thesis' where the explanation for why there is a stable order gives excessive importance to the role of ideological consensus. In actual fact, there is very widespread class (and no doubt other sources of) resentment which however is individualized and does lead on occasions to temporary and sporadic acts of individual and group resistance. It is not then the *acceptance* of the dominant ideology (even though, as Marx points out, the dominant ideas are the ideas of the ruling class) but the relative absence or weakness of efforts to bring together these scatter points of resentment and resistance that is the main, though not the only factor, that provides social order for the ruling classes.

24. Indeed, the vanguard party is an arena of initiative *and* of inertia. The institutionalized and bureaucratic routines that help to maintain organizational coherence and structure during normal times or in downturns become handicaps to overcome in periods of great upheaval. Unsurprisingly, factional fights, splits, inter-party bitterness may then occur.
25. The status of being a vanguard party has to be politically vindicated and its claims to representing the proletariat have to be democratically won. Can there be more than one vanguard party? The proletarian vanguard is itself a complex category. There is no stable hierarchy of working class interests and demands across time and space. It is highly unlikely therefore that any single political tendency can represent it at all times and for all its components and sections. Vanguard representation may or may

not be politically diverse. There could be a number of vanguard parties which come together in a common front. It could also be expressed through different tendencies within a single party or through some other appropriate combination. The exact forms are not so important as the fact that there should be mechanisms which can compensate and correct mistakes, rectify omissions in programme and struggle, ensure flexibility and speed of response.

26. Terry Eagleton is very good on this. See his 'Lenin in the Postmodern Age' in *Lenin Reloaded.*
27. E. Mandel, "Vanguard Parties" in *Bulletin in Defense of Marxism*, No. 44, September 1987. Mandel was a principal leader of the Fourth International (United Secretariat) which reflected in its internal workings the best traditions of the Bolshevik party when it had for a brief period full tendency rights and no ban on factions. The FI established further structures of democratic functioning and rules of internal discussion and practice in the 1960s and 70s in response to the rise of anti-racist and feminist movements.
28. The Iranian revolution was the biggest and most prolonged urban mass mobilization of history–literally millions repeatedly demonstrated over many months–that neutralized the fifth strongest army and one of the most feared secret service agencies (Savak) in the world.
29. D. Bensaid, 'Leaps, Leaps, Leaps' in *Lenin Reloaded*, p. 157.
30. A far right force in a liberal democratic framework can hope to rely on a gateway strategy to carry out its transformative project because its dominance in government does not threaten the essential character of bourgeois capitalist rule. The ruling class, however, will not be as sanguine when a genuinely revolutionary left force in government seeks not just to modify, but to decisively and permanently transform, the state structures that protect and sustain the rule of capital. Hence, the need for such a left to consider that relying *solely* on a gateway strategy can prove fatal.

APPENDIX

A Disastrous Judgement and a Huge Fillip for Hindutva

There have been two occasions when the Supreme Court (SC) has most grievously failed the people of India through its rulings. The first was in 1976 (ADM Jabalpur judgement) when our apex court—the supreme guardian of the 'Basic Structure' of the Constitution which includes the principles of secularism and democracy—declared that citizens have no resort to fundamental rights when there is a national emergency. The second occasion is now when a Constitutional bench comprising the five *senior most judges including the Chief Justice of India* gave a *unanimous* verdict on Ayodhya legitimising the utterly unjustifiable.

This ruling in fact deepens a dynamic that is much longer term and far more dangerous in its political impact and implications that that earlier one in 1976 legitimising Mrs. Gandhi's trashing of democracy during Emergency Rule. That declaration of Emergency was a desperate reaction to a much longer process of declining popularity of Mrs. Gandhi and more importantly of the Congress Party whose hegemony over Indian politics since 1947 had more or less ended by the late 1960s. Thereafter the Congress Party split with Mrs. Gandhi heading one wing still ensconced at the Centre, gaining temporary popularity because of victory over Pakistan in 1971-2 war, but in the years that followed facing tremendous loss of popularity because of domestic turmoil from a host of directions–the JP Movement against corruption, the 1974 nationwide Railway Strike, a judiciary that showed enough independence from the executive to indict Mrs. Gandhi for electoral foul play.

Emergency sought to reverse this political reality through coercive-administrative fiat. It didn't work. From the 1977 elections (held because Mrs. Gandhi mistakenly thought she would win and thus re-legitimise her rule) onwards, a new and prolonged phase of enormous electoral flux in Indian politics emerged. In its own way this constituted a certain crisis of unstable and uncertain bourgeois political leadership till the BJP/Sangh through its growing hegemony was finally able to present itself as the best candidate to act as saviour for the Indian capitalist ruling class. The current SC judgement is not a 'desperate reaction' to a ruling party's declining momentum but the very opposite. It actually expresses the reality of this expanding hegemonic drive and reinforces it! This verdict further emboldens the foot soldiers and the officials of the various organisations that are pushing the Hindutva agenda to more relentlessly and confidently pursue various other measures in their arsenal to help achieve the goal of a *Hindu Rashtra*.

The text that follows is divided into three parts and presented in a summary points form to make matters more concise and easier to read for left activists and supporters; and perhaps also for those liberals who have shown the political courage and integrity to unequivocally condemn the SC for this ruling and to recognise its very negative impact on India's political future, at least for some time to come. Unfortunately, there are far too many prominent liberal voices which have waffled on about the 'balance' and 'virtues' shown by the judgement even as some have expressed 'unease' at certain arguments. For them the sentiment in operation has been–"At long last we can leave behind this communally-divisive issue and the way is now cleared for us to collectively move forward to strengthen secularism and democracy in our resilient and remarkable nation."

We can be grateful that there are many others not willing to so delude themselves.

A

The Key Revelations and Crucial Conclusions Embodied in the Order

1. Exclusive title and possession given to the Hindu claimant of the *whole* of the site even as the SC admits that overall possession was *shared.*
2. To justify this, the SC declared that the Hindus had proportionately greater scope of possession because while they had exclusive possession of the outer courtyard Muslims only had shared possession of the inner courtyard where Hindus also worshipped. That there was an illegal incursion into the inner courtyard and mosque is noted, but carries no penalty in the final judgement. The fact that unlike the Hindus, Muslims never disrupted or damaged or evicted Hindu worshippers in the outer courtyard is, in legal terms counted against them, since it means that Hindus had exclusive possession. *The civility of Muslims is legally punished and the incivility and illegality of behaviour of Hindus is rewarded to the extent that the whole site is given to one side.*
3. (a) The SC acknowledges that the four centuries long gap between the dating of the underground remains that were archaeologically excavated and the construction of the Babri Masjid in 1528 makes it clear that no temple was destroyed in order to build the mosque. This is a rejection of the central claim and mobilising pivot of the hate-filled Ram Janamabhoomi campaign. Nowhere is it pointed out that this was a hateful and vicious campaign.

   (b) The SC acknowledges that in 1934 the dome of the mosque was damaged by Hindus.

   (c) The SC acknowledges that up to December 22/23, 1949 there was a functioning mosque.

(d) The SC acknowledges that on that night of 22/23 the mosque was illegally and criminally desecrated by the surreptitious placement of Hindu idols in the mosque.

(e) The SC acknowledges the criminality and illegality of the 1992 demolition of the mosque.

Despite all this, the SC, far from punishing has actually rewarded the side that endorsed this and benefitted from this illegality. Furthermore, this Order has not called for severe punishment of those identified as being in one way or the other involved in that demolition.

4. There is no escaping what is staring us in the face–*the only true course of justice would be demanding the full restoration/ rebuilding of a mosque.*
5. One judge (unnamed) added a lengthy addendum which declared that (a) there was a faith and belief stretching to before the beginning of the Common Era (CE) that Ayodhya was the site of the birth of Ram; (b) that Ram was not a mythical figure but an actual being and that furthermore oral and documentary evidence proves that the site was the birthplace of Ram. *It is extraordinary that given this violation of secular jurisprudence that a judge–and that too in a Constitution bench–sees fit to adjudicate on matters of the correctness or otherwise of faith and religious beliefs for the purposes of giving legal support to one side on a matter concerning a dispute over title and possession of land.*

B

The Reasons for Such SC Behaviour

1. Prior to the day of the ruling (November 10, 2019) massive security arrangements were made, and most importantly, spokespersons for the BJP/RSS/VHP and other organs of the Sangh Parivar, all insisted that the SC forthcoming verdict must be respected and accepted. There is no way a verdict going against the forces of Hindutva would ever have been

quietly accepted. It is more than highly probable that the Sangh leaders knew what was coming. How becomes the question that must be answered for the implications therein are extremely grave.

2. In fact everyone including the judges was aware that if there would be a verdict going against the Hindu claimants, then there would have been a massive explosion of organised and violent anger. The recognition of this reality no doubt also acted as a pressure on the judges. But political pragmatism cannot override issuing a judgement on the grounds of merit and true justice. The final verdict in favour of the forces of Hindutva cannot be justified on the grounds of political pragmatism.
3. Even if fear of negative and violent consequences was a major consideration far better than the final ruling would have been to follow one of two courses. (i) The bench could have ruled that the whole site would remain with the government and cleared of all worship and activity, while a mosque and a temple could be built outside the site itself. (ii) The judges could have mustered the courage to openly and transparently declare that political pragmatism and fear was a motivation for their final ruling; that this was a violation of justice and that this was a black day in the annals of Indian jurisprudence. Acknowledging what the proper and just verdict should have been and then giving their reasons for not taking this course would certainly on one hand be an act of cowardice but on the other hand, it would have shown a desire to maintain some clearly expressed degree of independence from the government which has allowed such an ugly reality to exist and giving a warning of the parlous political state of the country thereby providing some moral-political support for others fighting for secularism and democracy. *Instead the only conclusion to be drawn from the actual behaviour of the five senior most judges of the SC is a confirmation of how shamefully and deeply suborned this institution has now become to the forces of Hindutva.*

C

What Now to Politically Expect

1. A precedent has been set for Hindu groups to demand or even carry out the dismantling of other mosques which it is claimed are standing on land previously hallowed by having had temples or being otherwise sacred according to Hindu myths and beliefs. It would be utterly naïve to rule out future campaigns along these lines in other places such as Kashi and Mathura and elsewhere.
2. The rock-bottom principle of secular jurisprudence is that in any final confrontation faith cannot triumph over law. This has now been overturned. Furthermore, in the addendum things have gone further—here there has been the subordination of law to faith. A huge fillip has been given to the forces of Hindutva in their ongoing and determined effort to establish a *Hindu Rashtra* which necessarily requires a state that derives legal sanction (in lesser or greater measure) for having and sustaining a structural bias in favour of one religious community against another or other religious communities; in the case of India primarily against Muslims. The Citizenship Amendment Act, followed the Ayodhya judgement and the country-wide implantation of the National Register of Citizens has got further momentum as also the more general process through these and other forthcoming measures to more deeply and widely ghettoise, terrorise and inferiorise Muslims.
3. The construction of a 'grand' Ram Temple with official help and support from the Central and UP governments will begin shortly and both the pace of construction and the celebrations around the project will be carefully calibrated so as to maximise the possibility of electoral success whether at the assembly or central levels, the latter being due in 2024.
4. The suborning of the SC has been qualitatively enhanced.

5. The reactions of the opposition parties including of the CPM and CPI has been shameful. The Congress, SP, DMK, JD(S), AIIDMK, have all welcomed the verdict. Even the Dalit based party of Mayawati, the BSP, has welcomed the SC ruling. The BJD and TMC have refused to criticise the verdict which says enough. In their immediate responses the CPI called for peace and quiet acceptance of the verdict while the CPM has similarly called for a peaceful response and only suggested that there are some "questionable premises" in the arguments behind the arrival of the verdict. Neither of the two mainstream left parties has forthrightly condemned the ruling. In its immediate statement the CPI(ML)-Liberation also calls for harmony, does see "incoherence" in the arguments, but does not strongly condemn or unequivocally reject the ruling. It confines itself to saying that the verdict is "inconsistent and unconvincing" and will not resolve the dispute.

   A genuine Indian Left must be true to itself–independent, fearless and adopting a stand of uncompromising realism. This means we must neither underestimate the power of those ruling, nor accommodate ourselves to the powers that be. Only in this way can we take full and proper measure of our enemies, the better to prepare and fight for final victory.

Index